Stabilization and Reconstruction Staffing

Developing U.S. Civilian Personnel Capabilities

Terrence K. Kelly, Ellen E. Tunstall,
Thomas S. Szayna, Deanna Weber Prine

The research described in this report results from the RAND Corporation's continuing program of self-initiated research, which is made possible, in part, by the generous support of donors and by the independent research and development provisions of RAND's contracts for the operation of its U.S. Department of Defense federally funded research and development centers. The research was overseen by the RAND Arroyo Center Strategy, Doctrine, and Resources Program.

Library of Congress Cataloging-in-Publication Data

Stabilization and reconstruction staffing : developing U.S. civilian personnel capabilities / Terrence K. Kelly ... [et al.].
    p. cm.
    Includes bibliographical references.
    ISBN 978-0-8330-4137-1 (pbk. : alk. paper)
    1. Postwar reconstruction. 2. Personnel management—United States. 3. Human capital—United States—Management. I. Kelly, Terrence K. II. Rand Corporation.

JZ6374.S73 2008
353.1'5—dc22

                                                                        2007022780

The RAND Corporation is a nonprofit research organization providing objective analysis and effective solutions that address the challenges facing the public and private sectors around the world. RAND's publications do not necessarily reflect the opinions of its research clients and sponsors.

RAND® is a registered trademark.

Cover photo by U.S. Air Force Tech Sgt Jerry Morrison, Jr.

© Copyright 2008 RAND Corporation

Published 2008 by the RAND Corporation
1776 Main Street, P.O. Box 2138, Santa Monica, CA 90407-2138
1200 South Hayes Street, Arlington, VA 22202-5050
4570 Fifth Avenue, Suite 600, Pittsburgh, PA 15213-2665
RAND URL: http://www.rand.org/
To order RAND documents or to obtain additional information, contact
Distribution Services: Telephone: (310) 451-7002;
Fax: (310) 451-6915; Email: order@rand.org

Preface

The United States participated in several interventions and state-building efforts during the 1990s, and the rationale for U.S. engagement in such efforts received a new urgency after the 9/11 attacks. However, recent U.S. experiences in Afghanistan and, especially, in Iraq have shown that engaging in Security, Stability, Transition, and Reconstruction (SSTR) operations is a difficult and lengthy process that requires appropriate resources. Most of all, in order to have a chance of succeeding, a SSTR operation requires a realistic understanding of the capabilities needed for the operation.

This monograph presents the results of research on the U.S. civilian personnel and staffing programs for SSTR missions undertaken in other countries under U.S. leadership or with the participation of the United States. The study uses the Office of Personnel Management's Human Capital Assessment and Accountability Framework to assess the personnel requirements for such missions and presents recommendations that the U.S. government should undertake to deal with the types of problems that the United States has encountered in post-2003 Iraq. The research draws on the rapidly growing body of literature dealing with SSTR missions, interviews with U.S. and British civilian personnel deployed to Iraq, and the authors' own experiences in Iraq as U.S. civilians involved with the Coalition Provisional Authority. The study should be of interest to policymakers dealing with SSTR operations.

This research is part of RAND's continuing program of self-initiated research, which is made possible, in part, by the generous support of donors and by the independent research and development provisions of RAND's contracts for the operation of its U.S. Department of Defense federally funded research and development centers.

The research was overseen by the RAND Arroyo Center Strategy, Doctrine, and Resources Program. The RAND Arroyo Center is a federally funded research and development center sponsored by the U.S. Army. Additional information about RAND Arroyo Center is available at http://www.rand.org/ard/.

The views expressed in this monograph are those of the authors and do not reflect the official position of the U.S. Department of Defense or of the U.S. government.

Address comments and inquiries to Lauri Zeman, the director of the Strategy, Doctrine, and Resources Program, at Lauriz@rand.org, or 310-393-0411, extension 5524, or by mail at RAND Corporation, 1200 Hayes Street, Arlington, VA 22202-5050. Additional information about RAND is available at www.rand.org/.

Contents

Figures

Tables

Summary

Recent U.S. experiences in Afghanistan and Iraq have shown that engaging in Security, Stability, Transition, and Reconstruction (SSTR)[1] operations is a difficult and potentially lengthy process that requires appropriate resources. Most of all, in order to have a chance of being successful, a SSTR operation requires a realistic understanding of the capabilities needed for such an operation. This monograph examines one capability required for successful SSTR operations: the provision of competent civilian staffs that can manage and conduct the tasks needed for success.

The data gathered to support this research come from the rapidly growing body of literature dealing with SSTR missions and with how to increase the quality and quantity of civilian participation in recent SSTR operations; interviews with U.S. and British civilian personnel deployed to Iraq and personal correspondence with personnel having direct experience in SSTR operations or special visibility into the problems of civilian participation in SSTR operations; and the authors' own experiences in Iraq as U.S. civilians involved with the Coalition Provisional Authority (CPA). We used particularly the experiences of the CPA and its predecessor and successor organizations in Iraq, focusing on the ability of the United States to deploy such staffs to SSTR

---

[1] Since mid-2006, the Defense Department has used the term *Security, Stability, Transition, and Reconstruction* (SSTR) operations to refer to civilian-directed interagency efforts to stabilize a country that is undergoing some level of internal strife or lack of governance. We use the term for purposes of standardization.

operations and making recommendations to improve future SSTR operations.

This focus is motivated by the experiences of the CPA, which demonstrated that the United States failed, from several perspectives, to field a complete, competent civilian staff—an "A-Team." The staff could be characterized as short-term (few were there for longer than six months), and they were generally not what would be considered well-qualified. Almost none were experts on Iraq or the Middle East. Many worked in positions outside their professional expertise and well above the level of their previous experience. The failure to field an A-Team staff is not a criticism of the character or capabilities of any individual, nor of a lack of effort or competency on the part of those in leadership positions. Rather, it is an indictment of the lack of institutional capability.

The paradox of using civilians in SSTR efforts is that civilians usually move out of rather than into areas of political instability. A complete playbook for identifying, obtaining, and organizing human resources into an unstable area simply does not exist. However, there are statutes, rules, and policies that could facilitate future SSTR operations and provide a basis for identifying and recruiting candidates, assessing qualifications, appointing and compensating employees, and training and developing the workforce.

National-level policy and strategic direction should guide those charged with SSTR planning and operations, which include the creation of institutional pieces needed to implement policy. Planners should then use the U.S. Office of Personnel Management's (OPM's) Human Capital Assessment and Accountability Framework (HCAAF) and standards, developed as part of the President's Management Agenda,[2] to consider issues related to the creation and fielding of large

---

[2] "The President's Management Agenda (PMA) is a management initiative instituted by President George W. Bush in April 2001 to improve management practices across the Federal Government and transform government into results-oriented, efficient and citizen-centered enterprise" (U.S. Department of the Treasury, Office of Performance Budgeting and Strategic Planning, "About the President's Management Agenda." See Executive Office of the President, Office of Management and Budget, *The President's Management Agenda, Fiscal Year 2002*, Washington, D.C., no date.

civilian staffs. The Framework advocates strategic alignment, work-force planning and development, leadership and knowledge management, results-oriented performance culture, talent management, and accountability. See Figure S.1.

Policy and Strategic Direction

With regard to policy and strategic direction, policymakers should include human resources and resource managers when planning SSTR operations, to ensure that plans and policies are executable and that human resources and other organizations, especially budget and finance, actively support policy implementation.

Figure S.1
Fitting the Pieces Together

Strategic Alignment

Findings

To ensure strategic alignment, which, according to OPM, is a system "that promotes alignment of human capital management strategies with agency mission, goals, and objectives through analysis, planning, investment, measurement and management of human capital programs," it is imperative to determine how the operation will be managed at all levels. Many different agencies are part of the federal government, and each has its own human-resources (HR) functions and management systems, although all are loosely related under the OPM umbrella. That separateness leads to one key problem: achieving unity of effort. In particular, a SSTR operation will require a unified staff working to achieve the goals of the U.S. government, but it will almost certainly be populated by individuals from several departments and agencies, as well as by contractor personnel. In view of the issues that surfaced during our interviews, as well as our direct experience with the CPA, we chose three basic criteria for evaluating options on how to achieve a unity of effort:

1. **Responsiveness to the Ambassador:** The SSTR operation is likely to have small staffs that provide assistance to deployed personnel. Having a single organizational point of contact for personnel issues across government will be critical to success. The distinguishing characteristic of this criterion is an operational focus.

2. **Capacity and capability:** No single agency will have the breadth of contacts and expertise to recruit the best personnel in every required field. The goal of this criterion is to maximize the use of recruiting capabilities across the U.S. government.

3. **Accountability:** Spreading the responsibility for personnel functions across all involved departments and agencies with no formal mechanism that ensures accountability will lead to shortcomings in finding and fielding high-quality personnel and to accounting for those personnel while in theater. Although clearly related, accountability differs from responsive-

ness, in that *responsiveness* has to do with the ease of coordination between the Ambassador's staff and the HR organization supporting that staff's needs, whereas *accountability* has to do with the ability of the HR organization to document and manage the HR functions needed to support the fielded staff, as well as to measure the results of the HR process.

We examined three models that could provide a solution to achieving all three criteria for unity of effort: (1) one agency having responsibility for the personnel-management effort for the entire operation, (2) one agency leading, supported by the other agencies supplying personnel to the effort, and (3) decentralized recruiting, with agencies validating and filling specific billets in their assigned areas of responsibility as needed, but without central direction or control. The second model came out best, although it has some shortcomings in accountability.

Recommendations

- The President should direct the National Security Council and the OPM to chair a SSTR panel to study, among other things, who should lead SSTR human-resources planning and operations support, and, after considering the panel's recommendations, designate a lead agency for HR efforts and coordination across government.
- The lead HR office should then determine and document how it will support SSTR operations, and develop anticipated personnel requirements and costs.
- The President should request, and Congress should authorize, standing authority to recruit SSTR personnel and pay related personnel costs. Use of such authority and funds then should be subject only to an appropriate declaration of need by the President. These funds should be available to the lead HR agency, thus eliminating additional financial burdens on departments and agencies seconding personnel to a SSTR effort.

Workforce Planning

Findings

Workforce planning is a key component of strategic alignment and forms the basis for deploying civilians. Such planning should engage operational and HR experts to fully document (i.e., make sure there are job descriptions), and work with the responsible agencies to *validate* (i.e., formally determine that the position is needed and properly defined), staff requirements.

Recommendations

The resulting plan should be detailed but flexible. The State Department's Office of the Coordinator for Reconstruction and Stabilization (S/CRS) and the lead HR office should develop a notional workforce plan that planners could scale for larger operations or modify to meet unanticipated requirements. The plan should designate the agency responsible for each billet, time lines for filling positions, sources of candidates, and resource requirements and funding sources or responsibilities.

Talent Management, Performance Culture, Leader and Knowledge Management

Findings

The last three elements of HCAAF—talent management, performance culture, and leader and knowledge management—deal with who actually fills what position, as well as with HR and SSTR operational issues. Critical to these elements are recruiting and retaining staff, intellectual and experiential capital, and performance expectations and results. For example, under leadership and knowledge management, the Departments of State and Defense have each begun to address aggressively the types of leadership and continuity gaps that were articulated by many of our interviewees. For example, the State Department's Strategic Plan for 2007 indicates that the Department will increase the percentage of language-designated positions at overseas missions filled by people who fully meet language requirements and will mandate leadership and management training for 100 percent of its targeted population.[3]

Recommendations

The lead HR agency, in coordination with responsible agencies and OPM, should

- determine what, if any, inducements are necessary to attract and retain needed personnel for SSTR operations.
- consider options such as signing bonuses, specialty pay, and retirement and promotion benefits, as well as specialty training.
- provide participants with information and intelligence on world hot spots as permitted by their need-to-know and security clearances.

Furthermore, S/CRS and OPM should conduct a gap analysis to compare existing authorities to staffing requirements to determine what, if any, additional authorities or legislation is needed to ensure that recruiting and retention efforts will result in a full, competent staff that is well prepared to execute the mission.

Conclusion

If the United States is to succeed in future SSTR efforts, the U.S. government must put human-resources considerations at the center of its planning efforts, include the human-resources community as a full and ongoing partner, and modernize legislative and policy considerations in order to field an A-Team. There is much at stake: If the United States ever again undertakes a SSTR operation requiring a large civilian staff and finds itself reinventing on the fly the systems by which such a staff will be created and populated, the likely result will be a significant waste of resources and possibly of lives.

---

[3] U.S. Department of State and U.S. Agency for International Development, "Strategic Goal Chapter 12: Management and Organizational Excellence," *FY 2007 Joint Performance Summary*, Washington, D.C., no date.

Acknowledgments

The authors acknowledge the many dedicated Americans and allies who have served in civilian staffs during SSTR operations in the recent past, particularly in the Balkans, Afghanistan, and Iraq. This monograph is meant to make their and their successors' tasks easier and more successful. The hardships they and their families bear, as well as the personal danger they face, are underreported and underappreciated. On April 23, 1910, former President Theodore Roosevelt said in a speech given at the Sorbonne in Paris, France:[1]

> It is not the critic who counts; not the man who points out how the strong man stumbles, or where the doer of deeds could have done them better. The credit belongs to the man who is actually in the arena, whose face is marred by dust and sweat and blood; who strives valiantly; who errs, who comes short again and again, because there is no effort without error and shortcoming; but who does actually strive to do the deeds; who knows great enthusiasms, the great devotions; who spends himself in a worthy cause; who at the best knows in the end the triumph of high achievement, and who at the worst, if he fails, at least fails while daring greatly, so that his place shall never be with those cold and timid souls who neither know victory nor defeat.

This quote sums up the efforts of many great people who have spent portions of their lives, and sometimes have lost their lives, help-

---

[1] Theodore Roosevelt, "'The Man in the Arena' Speech at the Sorbonne, Paris, France, April 23, 1910," *Citizenship in a Republic.*

ing their country and the people of devastated parts of the world. We hope this monograph will make future SSTR operations more successful, and dedicate it to these great men and women.

We would also like to thank the many people who agreed to talk with us while we prepared this monograph, and in particular former Coalition Provisional Authority officials David Gompert, Larry Crandall, Fred Smith, Tom Foley, Paul Schulte, Phil Jamison, Dave Brannan, and Larry Diamond, as well as many others too numerous to mention. We would also like to thank Julia Taft, Chris Hoe, Joe Benkert, Don Krumm, John Heffern, Tex Harris, Nancy Kichak, George Nesterczuk, Marilee Fitzgerald, and the many other current or former government officials who made this document possible. Finally, Jerry Sollinger, Mary Debold, Terri Perkins, and Patrice Lester of RAND contributed to the exposition and professional presentation of this monograph, and made it possible in real ways. We thank them for their efforts.

We also thank Hans Binnendijk at the National Defense University and Douglas Brook at the Naval Postgraduate School for their thoughtful reviews of an earlier draft of this monograph.

To the extent that there are errors or shortcomings in this monograph, the authors bear sole responsibilities for them.

Abbreviations

ACT	Advanced Civilian Team
AWC	Army War College
CAC	Common Access Card
CFR	Code of Federal Regulations
CJTF-7	Combined Joint Task Force–Seven
CMPT	Civil-Military Planning Team
COG	Continuity of Government
COOP	Continuity of Operations
CPA	Coalition Provisional Authority
CRS	Office of the Coordinator for Reconstruction and Stabilization
CRSG	Country Reconstruction and Stabilization Group
DART	Disaster Assistance Response Team
DDR	Demilitarization, Demobilization and Reintegration
DFID	Department for International Development (UK)

DoD	Department of Defense
EU	European Union
FCO	Foreign and Commonwealth Office (UK)
FSO	Foreign Service Officer
GAO	Government Accountability Office
HCAAF	Human Capital Assessment and Accountability Framework
HR	Human Resources
HRST	Humanitarian, Reconstruction and Stability Team
IC	Intelligence Community
ICITAP	International Crime Investigative Training Assistance Program
ICS	Iraqi Correctional Service
IDA	Institute for Defense Analyses
IFI	International Financial Institution
IO	International Organization
IPA	Intergovernmental Personnel Act
IPC	Integration Planning Cell
IRC	Iraqi Correctional Service
IRDC	Iraq Reconstruction and Development Council
JFCOM	Joint Forces Command
JMD	Joint Manning Document
KBR	Kellogg, Brown and Root

MNSTC-I	Multi-National Security Transition Command–Iraq
MoD	Ministry of Defense
MOI	Ministry of Interior
NATO	North Atlantic Treaty Organization
NDU	National Defense University
NGO	Nongovernmental Organization
NSC	National Security Council
NSPD	National Security Presidential Directive
OIF	Operation Iraqi Freedom
OMB	Office of Management and Budget
ONSA	Office of National Security Affairs
OPM	Office of Personnel Management
ORHA	Office of Reconstruction and Humanitarian Assistance
OSCE	Organization for Security and Cooperation in Europe
OSD	Office of the Secretary of Defense
PCC	Policy Coordinating Committee
PCRU	Post-Conflict Reconstruction Unit
PDD	Presidential Decision Directive
PSD	Personal Security Detachment
RCC	Regional Combatant Command
RMOA	Resource Management Organization Analysis

S/CRS	State Department's Office of the Coordinator for Reconstruction and Stabilization
S&R	Stability and Reconstruction
SES	Senior Executive Service
SRC	Standing Reserve Corps
SRO	Stability and Reconstruction Operation
SSTR	Security, Stability, Transition, and Reconstruction
TR	Transition and Reintegration
UK	United Kingdom
UN	United Nations
UNDP	United Nations Development Programme
USAID	U.S. Agency for International Development
USG	U.S. government

CHAPTER ONE

The Problem

The United States . . . tends to staff each new operation as if it were its first and destined to be its last. Service in such missions has never been regarded as career enhancing for American military or Foreign Service officers. Whereas the United Nations, despite a generally dysfunctional personnel system, has gradually built up a cadre of experienced nation-builders, including several retired senior U.S. officials, the United States starts each mission more or less from scratch. Whereas the United Nations established a Best Practices unit in its Peacekeeping Department to study and adopt lessons learned in prior operations in 1995, the U.S. Department of State created a similar unit only in 2004.[1]

When President George W. Bush declared the end of major combat operations in Iraq on May 1, 2003, the U.S. government expected and planned for a short, caretaker occupation leading to a quick, clean departure. During the next six months, the Office of Reconstruction and Humanitarian Assistance (ORHA), and then the Coalition Provisional Authority (CPA), came to grips with the fact that, rather than acting as a short-term, caretaker government, it would have to be the government, design and create an Iraqi governmental structure, recruit government leaders (in the case of the Ministry of Defense, an entire

---

[1] James Dobbins, Seth G. Jones, Keith Crane, Andrew Rathmell, Brett Steele, Richard Teltschik, and Anga Timilsina, *The UN's Role in Nation-Building: From the Congo to Iraq*, Santa Monica, Calif.: RAND Corporation, MG-304-RC, 2005, p. 247.

ministry), and train and advise that government, all while facing a rising level of violence from a variety of sources.[2]

Over the 7-1/2 months between November 15, 2003, when the coalition agreed to return sovereignty to Iraq, and June 28, 2004, when the CPA closed down, its staffing documents called for almost 3,000 members, most of whom were civilians.[3] However, one former member of the Office of Policy, Planning and Analysis of the CPA estimates that personnel on hand never topped 55 percent of the requirement, whereas the Government Accountability Office (GAO) reported that about a third of the needed positions were not filled.[4] In finding people for that staff, the CPA, and its parent organizations and the Department of Defense (DoD), had to answer basic human-resources questions, including:

- Which billets are to be filled from government departments and agencies, and which from the private sector?
- What skills are needed?
- What billets, if any, must be filled with U.S. personnel?
- What billets, if any, should be filled with political appointees?

---

[2] ORHA and then the CPA faced a number of insurgencies, criminal efforts, and other sources of violence, all occurring simultaneously.

[3] There was no one CPA manning document; rather, a dynamic spreadsheet was maintained in Washington with input from Baghdad. The implication of not having formal requirements that drive personnel recruiting will be discussed subsequently. It does not appear that a clear articulation of the final requirement for staff was ever produced, which precluded these requirements being validated and filled.

[4] Email exchange with former CPA staff responsible for maintaining CPA statistics for Ambassador L. Paul Bremer. Different reports indicate different percentages of personnel in place. For example, a Government Accountability Office (GAO) report from June 2004 (*Rebuilding Iraq: Resource, Security, Governance, Essential Services, and Oversight Issues*) indicates that staffing never topped two-thirds of the requirement. However, this same report indicates much smaller numbers of required personnel than do other sources. See Table A.1 in the Appendix for a summary of the numbers reported by the GAO. We note as well that the *Personnel Assessment Team Report to the Secretary of Defense* (U.S. Department of Defense, 2004) at one point asserts that 68 percent of authorized positions were filled. But this statistic includes some military personnel, and it fails to include several hundred additional authorized personnel not yet added to the roster.

- How long are personnel to stay in Iraq? How much should they be paid?

Bearing out the contrasts in the above quote, several instances of the shortcomings of the U.S. effort illustrate problems that involved staffing: the abilities of the staff in the field, the ability of offices back in the states to continue to function because of staffing shortages, and the ability to match staff experience with that perceived as being appropriate by indigenous leaders. For example,

- members of a personnel-evaluation team that visited the CPA in January 2004 characterized the staff as a pickup organization in place to design and execute the most demanding transformation in recent U.S. history.
- bureaucratic and tactical considerations of running some individual offices within DoD caused some office directors to actively discourage personnel from joining the CPA and overshadowed the strategic goal of achieving success in Iraq.
- in many cultures (such as those in the Middle East), age, seniority, and gender indicate gravitas and importance. Young, inexperienced people in senior jobs are not taken seriously or, worse, are perceived as showing a lack of seriousness on the part of the United States.

Background

The United States has intervened in other countries and has conducted state-building efforts for well over a century.[5] Most recently, it participated in several interventions and state-building efforts during the 1990s to aid in controlling the consequences of state breakdown. The rationale for U.S. engagement in peace-building and state-building efforts received a new urgency after the attacks of September

---

[5] The Mexican War may be the first large-scale intervention, but certainly from the time of the Spanish-American War and U.S. deployments to Cuba and the Philippines this has been a task the United States has taken on with some frequency.

11, 2001 (9/11), with the recognition that the confluence of poor governance and underdevelopment makes possible the growth of radical movements and transnational criminal networks that either target the United States or act against U.S. interests. Both the peace operations of the 1990s and the stability operations in the post-9/11 era demonstrate the pressures that the United States and its allies are under to control political instability in the developing countries, improve those countries' capacity for governance, and deal with the international consequences of intrastate strife and violence.

However, recent U.S. experiences in Afghanistan and, especially, in Iraq have shown that engaging in Stability and Reconstruction Operations, now called Stability, Security, Transition, and Reconstruction (SSTR),[6] is a difficult and lengthy process that requires appropriate resources. Most of all, to have a chance of being successful, a stability operation requires a realistic understanding of the capabilities needed for the operation.

Purpose and Scope

This monograph examines one capability required for successful SSTR operations: the provision of competent civilian staffs that can manage and conduct the tasks needed for success. More specifically, it examines the process of determining civilian staffing requirements and ways of meeting those requirements. The focus on the staffing process is shaped by the Human Capital Assessment and Accountability Framework (HCAAF), a guide developed by the Office of Personnel Management (OPM) and the Office of Management and Budget (OMB) in response to the President's Management Agenda,[7] and by U.S. government–wide concern about the strategic management of human capital.

---

[6] Since mid-2006, the Defense Department has used the term *Security, Stability, Transition, and Reconstruction* (SSTR) operations to refer to civilian-directed interagency efforts to stabilize a country that is undergoing some level of internal strife or lack of governance. We use the term for purposes of standardization.

[7] "The President's Management Agenda (PMA) is a management initiative instituted by President George W. Bush in April 2001 to improve management practices across the Fed-

The authors' first-hand experiences with the Coalition Provisional Authority in Iraq made it obvious to them that the United States failed to field a complete, competent civilian staff. That assessment has been echoed widely by others familiar with the CPA experience.[8] It is not a criticism of the capabilities of any individual who worked for the CPA—the authors believe that, for the most part, these were extraordinary people of real talent. Furthermore, the U.S. failure in this regard should not be attributed to a lack of effort or competency on the part of those charged with the task or to their leadership abilities. Rather, it simply states that the staff, as a staff, was inadequate.

The failure was in institutional capability rather than in individual effort: The United States simply does not have, organized and in place, the bureaucratic machinery and expertise necessary to field large, competent civilian staffs for SSTR operations quickly. And, although the research reported here is not a postmortem of the CPA, that experience highlights the need, and serves as an impetus and a starting point, for examining the challenge of how to field competent civilian staffs in future SSTR operations.

In conducting this research, it was also necessary to consider the context in which SSTR operations could take place—that is, the magnitude of the U.S. commitment and the U.S. role in the overall effort (whether the United States is participating as part of a standing international body's efforts, alone, or as part of an ad hoc coalition). The United States realistically cannot plan to create and field SSTR staffs that are, in effect, unbounded in size or undefined in composition or role. Situations requiring very large commitments (e.g., such as those

---

eral Government and transform government into results-oriented, efficient and citizen-centered enterprise" (U.S. Department of the Treasury, Office of Performance Budgeting and Strategic Planning, "About the President's Management Agenda." See Executive Office of the President, Office of Management and Budget, *The President's Management Agenda, Fiscal Year 2002*, Washington, D.C., no date).

[8] The inadequacy of the CPA staff as a staff is acknowledged by all of its former members interviewed for this research, as well as by two of the authors, one of whom held a senior position on the CPA staff and the other of whom was the deputy leader of DoD's Personnel Assessment Team of the CPA (*Personnel Assessment Team Report to the Secretary of Defense*, February 2004).

undertaken in Germany after World War II) are not considered here, because such operations would require programs and efforts not called for in any but the most extraordinary circumstances.

Nonetheless, the U.S. government must identify its requirements for SSTR capabilities before it can consider the size of, and resources to be committed to, creating civilian SSTR staffing capabilities. As of the completion of this monograph, we are not aware of an effort by the U.S. government to do so in a definitive fashion; therefore, we make some assumptions about how such requirements can be identified, based on our first-hand experience with CPA and current government efforts.

The research and analysis for this project began in late 2004 and ended in January 2006. A draft version of this monograph was completed in May 2006. After a formal review process, the monograph was revised and updated selectively. The report was cleared for public release in April 2007.

Approach

Our main research question is: What steps can the U.S. government take to develop the capability to provide competent civilian support to SSTR operations? To address the question, we use a four-step approach:

- Define core descriptors of a competent SSTR staff, as well as a framework for articulating requirements for adequate staff.
- Examine approaches for filling staffing requirements.
- Articulate the legal, policy, and human concerns and challenges of creating the capabilities needed for these approaches.
- Put forth a set of options for creating these capabilities in the U.S. government.

The data gathered to support this research come from two sources: (1) literature on how to increase the quality and quantity of civilian participation in recent SSTR operations and (2) interviews and personal correspondence with personnel having direct experience in SSTR operations or special visibility into the problems of civilian participation in SSTR operations. We chose people to interview according to their

- experiences with the CPA or other SSTR deployments
- knowledge of current scholarship on SSTR and efforts similar to SSTR
- current involvement with U.S. or United Kingdom (UK) SSTR policy, plans, or programmatic development
- insights into how other organizations, such as the United Nations (UN), conduct SSTR efforts
- experience with U.S. federal government personnel systems.

We limited the scope of our literature review to the debate on how to find a solution to the problem, and we seek to contribute to that debate. Our review of the literature on addressing the shortcomings in fielding civilian staffs in recent SSTR operations covered primarily U.S. government documents and analysis at policy-focused research organizations, such as the United States Institute of Peace or the Carnegie Endowment for International Peace. Policy briefings and research reports made up most of the literature that we surveyed as part of this effort. We understand that the discussions that are part of this debate are underpinned by and rely on insights found in the literature on public administration and management, although the research reported here does not include a survey of the academic literature on the topic.

As to interview data, we considered the expertise and insights of personnel with direct and extensive experience in SSTR and humanitarian aid efforts. The interviewees included those with experience in the U.S. government as well as those with experience in international organizations (IOs), Nongovernmental Organizations (NGOs), or the private sector. The interviewees included 18 experts who either held senior positions during recent SSTR operations (e.g., CPA Senior Advisors, former U.S. Agency for International Development [USAID] Mission Directors) or had experience with government or international bodies involved in SSTR operations (e.g., with the State Department's Office of the Coordinator for Reconstruction and Stabilization [S/CRS]), USAID, the U.S. Institute of Peace, UN Development Program). In addition, we had formal and informal discussions and communications (including electronic-mail correspondence) with mid-level experts and practitioners with similar background and experience. The research also considers the insights of human-resources policy experts at the U.S. Office of Personnel Management, whom we included because this is their area of expertise.

The diverse set of interviewees led us to develop an informal and flexible set of questions, designed to pursue topics that the interviewee identified as important. In fact, we conducted the interviews more along the lines of structured discussions (open-ended questions, focusing on constructive suggestions for change). The general categories pursued in all the interviews were (1) direct experience pertaining to the role of civilian staff in SSTR operations; (2) identification and assessment of major problems with the civilian staff in SSTR operations; and (3) awareness and evaluation of ongoing efforts to address the issues identified. To ensure candid responses, we conducted all of the interviews, discussions, and communications on a not-for-attribution basis.

Finally, the authors have direct, relevant experience. Kelly was the Director for Militia Transition and Reintegration for the CPA from January 2004 until the CPA went out of existence at the end of June 2004. Tunstall was the principal director for DoD's civilian personnel policy community, as well as the deputy leader of the panel created by the Secretary of Defense to examine the personnel situation at the CPA.

Detailed data that would allow for a more informed assessment and analysis of the civilian staff in the CPA either were not available at the time we conducted the research (at least we were not able to obtain them) or were missing. Therefore, we relied heavily on interview data and on our own experience in the course of our research. We acknowledge our reliance on such "soft" data, but it is our impression that the kind of data we use was the best available at the time we conducted our research. We would welcome the publication of detailed data on skill sets of CPA civilian staff and the selection process of CPA civilians. The above caveat underpins the entire study.

The problem of inefficient and inadequate civilian participation in SSTR operations is widely acknowledged, but the extent of discussion of solutions is still in its early stage. It is one of the goals of this research effort to provide ideas on solutions and to draw the attention of the policy community to the possibility that, if the United States again undertakes a SSTR operation that requires a large civilian staff yet uses ad hoc measures and processes to put such a staff together, then the likely result will be a significant amount of resources wasted and lives endangered.

Organization

The remainder of this monograph contains four chapters and an appendix. Chapter Two describes the type of staff necessary for an Iraq-like SSTR operation and discusses briefly some of the shortcomings of the U.S. staff fielded in Iraq in 2003–2004. Chapter Three considers what types of capabilities the United States might need for SSTR operations and offers a framework for considering the supply and demand sides of the personnel equation. Chapter Four turns to what the U.S. government might be able to do to create a mechanism for fielding staffs for SSTR operations, reviews statutory and regulatory powers, and discusses ways to structure, manage, and implement a structure to field a competent civilian SSTR staff when the need arises. Chapter Five offers some recommendations and conclusions. The Appendix describes the historical experience in Iraq in creating a large staff for SSTR operations.

CHAPTER TWO

Motivation and Approaches

An authoritative study on the CPA experience remains to be written. However, the basic problems that surfaced with the civilians deployed to the CPA—i.e., the inadequacy of the civilian staff as a staff—are widely acknowledged. The organizational and procedural problems that prevented the deployment of what in colloquial terms might be called the "A-Team" (a group of top-notch experts put together for a specific mission) to Iraq have led to efforts within the U.S. government to deal with the identified shortcomings and to prevent their recurrence. This chapter addresses the shortcomings of the civilian staff deployed in support of the CPA. We describe briefly some of the organizational changes in the United States and the United Kingdom to field civilian SSTR staffs. In themselves, these efforts indicate a recognition of the problems encountered with the CPA.

The CPA Experience—Where Was the "A-Team"?

The consistent observation from all our interviews and direct experience with the CPA has two parts: (1) CPA experience illustrates well the importance of having the capability to create large, competent staffs for critical SSTR efforts; (2) the CPA did not have such a staff in place.

One could characterize the CPA staff as short-term (few were there for longer than six months) and not what would generally be considered well qualified for the work they were tasked to do. Almost none were experts on Iraq or the Middle East, many were working in positions outside of their area of professional expertise, and many were working far above the level of their previous experience. This was true not only of the junior and mid-level staff members, but also of some senior staff.[1]

Members of a competent civilian staff for a SSTR operation (an "A-Team") should have the following traits or provide the following benefits:

1. Provide continuity (i.e., are in country for at least one year).
2. Work in their areas of professional and technical expertise.
3. Work at a level not grossly beyond their previous experiences (some amount of "working up" is to be expected in situations such as these).
4. Include an appropriate number of experts on the part of the world in which the operation is to take place.
5. Have the temperament and ability to work in a location that is austere and, at times, dangerous (i.e., have the "psychological fitness" required for these situations).

It is clear that the United States did not field an "A-Team" in Iraq, because none of these five traits was addressed satisfactorily.

CPA personnel records are sparse, incomplete, and spread out across the government. Consequently, we lack the statistical data to describe fully the situation on the ground. That said, the interview data we obtained and our direct experience are unanimous in supporting our general assessment that an "A-Team" did not deploy. Members of a personnel-evaluation team that visited the CPA in January 2004 characterized the staff as a pickup organization in place to design and

---

[1] Temporary senior CPA employees were not members of the Senior Executive Service. The Senior Executive Service (SES) was established by subchapter II of Chapter 31, Title 5, United States Code, which provides the compensation, benefits, incentives, and other conditions of employment for senior executives in the federal government. Temporary CPA employees were not covered by these provisions, and so they cannot be considered members of the SES. However, many held positions with responsibilities commensurate with those of the SES and received equivalent pay ($109,808 to $165,200 in calendar year 2005) (see the U.S. Office of Personnel Management Web site).

execute the most demanding transformation in recent U.S. history[2]—a symptom of the fact that no machinery was in place to deploy non-military personnel to areas such as Iraq; thus, the staff was inadequate as a staff. Interviews with former CPA officials, as well as the experiences of the principal author who served with the CPA, also highlight the extent of the problem. For example, the Office of Security Affairs, later renamed the Office of National Security Affairs, contained only one person willing to stay for a year (the Senior Advisor's executive assistant).[3] Others stayed from three to nine months, with the average being less than six months.[4] The office of the advisors to the Ministry of Interior (MOI) had similar longevity, with only four out of a total requirement of 281 (the top number authorized, although the advisory team to the MOI never had more than 68 people) staying for a year.[5] Ambassador L. Paul Bremer's Office of Planning and Policy Assessment did not have anyone staying for a year.[6]

Evidence about the other descriptors of an A-Team member also indicates severe problems. With regard to experience, the Office of National Security Affairs was, among other things, charged with building the Iraqi Ministry of Defense (MoD) from scratch, advising Ambassador Bremer on strategic-level security issues, establishing a stipend program for form soldiers of Saddam's army, and establishing the policy and programs for, and negotiating agreements to, transition and reintegrate (TR) Iraqi militiamen out of their armed organizations into civil society. Although the MoD effort was competently led, some of the staff members involved in it lacked the appropriate qualifications and background. For example, two of the three U.S. personnel working on the project were missile-defense experts rather than experts in the areas they were charged with—

---

[2] Tunstall's recollection as deputy team leader.

[3] We note that many qualified people volunteered to go to Iraq, but almost none volunteered to deploy for a year.

[4] Kelly's observations and recollections as a member of this office from January to June 2004.

[5] Email from former senior CPA official, May 2005.

[6] Interviews with senior CPA officials, April–May 2005.

personnel and training. The individual charged with the militia TR effort was a U.S. homeland-security expert. The Director for National Security, whose charge was advising the senior director on the whole range of Iraqi security issues, was a former professional tennis player with limited government security experience.

There are similar stories about the experiential base of people in other key positions. One key advisor to the Senior Advisor for National Security Affairs was a graduate student who had never held a job related to her task. The representative from the CPA Office of Management and Budget for the militia TR effort was similarly inexperienced. Senior advisors—the executives responsible for large sections of the CPA, and who usually reported directly to Ambassador Bremer—were often very junior. Individuals who would have held junior to mid-level civil service positions were thrust into positions that should have been staffed by members of the SES or other executive cadre (e.g., the Senior Foreign Service).

Finally, very few Iraq experts were on the CPA staff until late in the CPA's tenure. The Office of National Security Affairs (ONSA) had no Iraq or Middle Eastern experts; the same could be said for almost every office in the CPA. These people were, by and large, very talented and worked tremendously hard, but did not have appropriate backgrounds to make many of the decisions required of the CPA (e.g., selecting general officers for the Iraqi military and senior members of the MoD—coalition authorities made their decisions based on resumes and interviews, but without deep insights into the backgrounds, qualifications, and motivations of the individuals under consideration).

Dissatisfaction with Human-Resources Processes and Procedures

We note that there may have been many reasons behind the failure to field an A-Team. Much of what was done in Iraq falls outside normal government functions. Without a program in place to recruit and retain people with such unusual skills as creating government structures from scratch, excavating mass graves, mediating ethnic and sectarian disputes, or disbanding party militias, the U.S. government could not have expected to have the right people on hand when needed. Furthermore, the contentious political nature of Operation Iraqi Freedom and the subsequent occupation may have discouraged many potential A-Team members who may have had such skills.[7] A lack of effective intergovernmental or general public recruiting for people to join the CPA despite the authority to do so under National Security Presidential Directive (NSPD) 24 also could have contributed to the failure to field an A-Team.[8]

Furthermore, the CPA needed people quickly, and surge hiring is not the norm for federal human-resources (HR) offices. In fact, at the time of this research effort, the conversation across government and among Chief Human Capital Officers was how to speed up the hiring process and make the most use of the flexibilities available. Owing in part to widespread dissatisfaction with federal human-resources processes and procedures, it is no surprise that the responsibility for staffing the CPA originally resided outside of DoD's civilian personnel community (the CPA set up its own personnel effort, which operated independently of existing systems) or that there was little effective outreach across the federal HR community. The cost of military operations overshadowed the requirement to adequately address and fund civilian programs, which also contributed to the overall hiring problem.

Capacity

The existence of personnel systems that could have produced additional qualified staff members but did not goes directly to the question of capacity. Specifically, personnel systems in each department and agency of the U.S. government operate under OPM or agency rules to bring qualified people into federal service. It is an indication of a critical failure that the collective personnel systems of the U.S. government, which involve approximately 2.7 million employees, did not find an additional 2,000 to 3,000 well-qualified people who would deploy to Iraq.

---

[7] Interview with a retired Senior Foreign Service Officer, October 21, 2004.

[8] Discussions in August 2004 with the head of one U.S. government agency indicated that he was not even aware there was a need for volunteers.

According to the GAO, although the total number of CPA employees fluctuated, the composition of personnel, on average, remained relatively constant:[9]

- Approximately 28 percent of the staff members was military personnel.
- Approximately 13 percent was from other coalition countries.
- Approximately 26 percent was civilians from numerous U.S. government agencies, including the Department of Defense.
- About 25 percent was contractors and temporary employees hired under Section 3161 of Title 5, United States Code (5 USC 3161).

These statistics indicate that the U.S. government supplied just over half (26 percent from U.S. government agencies and 25 percent from temporary hires) of those actually deployed under its mode of operation for Iraq and used other sources to field the rest of its staff, including military manpower and contributions from allies and coalition partners. As a percentage of need, the number is actually far lower, considering that at its maximum the CPA was never staffed to its articulated requirement.[10]

To begin to understand why the U.S. government did not recruit the needed personnel requires a basic understanding of how federal government personnel systems work. Government personnel systems respond to *documented* (i.e., a job description exists) and *validated* (i.e., a formal determination that the position is needed and properly defined) requirements placed on them by their parent agencies. Specifically, a validated request that describes a position (e.g., skills required, grade

---

[9] U.S. Government Accountability Office (GAO), *Rebuilding Iraq: Resource, Security, Governance, Essential Services, and Oversight Issues*, Report to Congressional Committees, Washington, D.C.: GAO-04-902-R, June 2004.

[10] These requirements were often not validated, thus putting no demand on the U.S. government personnel systems. GAO numbers do not add to 100 percent; the report provides no explanation about the supplier of the residual 8 percent of personnel. Furthermore, as noted previously, estimates are that the CPA staff was never above 58 percent of requirements, indicating that the civilian personnel system never produced more than approximately 28 percent of the required personnel.

level, duration) sets in motion the machinery to advertise for and hire someone to fill that billet, which may include candidates from within the government personnel system, as well as from the private sector. The fact that the CPA was a temporary organization with no defined staffing roster, and therefore no documented and validated requirements, to some extent explains why government personnel systems did not supply the needed staff.

Volunteers

The performance of U.S. government personnel systems also raises another important issue: Why did government employees, particularly those from DoD, which was the parent organization for the CPA, not volunteer to go to Iraq in larger numbers? Indeed, interviews with career DoD employees indicate that not only did DoD offices not encourage people to volunteer, but some offices actually discouraged them from going and denied them benefits, such as overtime pay, afforded to government employees from other agencies.[11] Similarly, an employee from a domestic U.S. government agency described his agency's elaborate efforts to keep him from deploying at all, as well as its concerted efforts to make him return before the end of his tour with the CPA.[12] Apparently, the bureaucratic and tactical organizational considerations of running some individual offices within DoD overshadowed the U.S. strategic policy goal of achieving success in Iraq.

More generally, our research indicates that there were no governmentwide policies for recruiting and retaining personnel from within the government for duty with the CPA, and even that some departments and agencies, to include DoD, either did not have uniform policies and procedures for personnel matters (e.g., overtime, bonuses), or did not apply them. Furthermore, there does not appear to have been a single human-resources office charged with managing the totality of HR functions for the CPA, which was instead managed from the temporary office established in the Pentagon (CPA Rear) with assistance

---

[11] Interviews with two OSD employees, October 2004.

[12] Interview with a U.S. government employee, October 2004.

from the Army's HR community. CPA Rear also provided the full spectrum of support to the field.

Understanding the Problem

Unless institutional problems are fixed and needed capability developed, some of the reasons for the failure of the personnel system to staff the CPA properly may plague future U.S. operations as well. Understanding the problem begins with that simple observation—the U.S. A-Team did not go to Iraq—and with the facts that the U.S. government's efforts to get the word out, provide incentives, or use other means to get a competent staff to Iraq did not work. Furthermore, SSTR operations are not short-term. If it is to be successful in future SSTR operations, the U.S. government needs to be able to field not only an A-Team when it needs it, but also to replace that A-Team with a second A-Team, followed by a third and perhaps subsequent A-Teams for long, multiyear efforts.[13] Additionally, the need to maintain a competent staff over a potentially long period is one of the considerations that influences the manner—if not the size—of conducting SSTR operations taken on by the United States.

Ongoing Steps to Address the Problem

The inability of the United States (and its allies and coalition partners) to field large, competent staffs has been widely recognized. Below, we summarize the U.S. and UK approaches to fielding SSTR capabilities in late 2005, when this research concluded, focusing on those elements directly relevant to this research. The organizational process is moving along rapidly in the United States, although creating an adequate civilian staff remains among the most difficult and yet central aspects to developing a genuine interagency, coordinated response capability for SSTR operations.

---

[13] Note that the composition and size of staffs after the first iteration may vary significantly, depending on the success of initial efforts. The duration of deployments and the issue of changing staff requirements are discussed below.

The United Nations has great capabilities for planning and conducting many components of SSTR operations (e.g., humanitarian operations; demobilization, demilitarization, and reintegration of combatants; establishment of governance structures). It relies primarily on the contributions of member states and *ad hoc* hiring to staff its efforts, although, as an organization in its own right, it brings significant technical expertise to such operations. In the following subsections, we describe efforts by U.S. and UK participants in UN operations to put in place coordinated interagency efforts.

U.S. Efforts

U.S. participation in several peace operations during the 1990s demonstrated a need for a coordinated interagency effort that would be in place in the aftermath of an intervention intended to stabilize a country. Presidential Decision Directive 56 (PDD-56), issued in 1997,[14] established a strong role for the National Security Council (NSC) and a structure for such coordination. With the change of administrations after the 2000 elections, the effort ended, although the post–Operation Iraqi Freedom (OIF) efforts to provide for better interagency coordination in SSTR operations revived some of the ideas in PDD-56. NSPD-44, on Management of Interagency Efforts Concerning Reconstruction and Stabilization, signed in December 2005, superseded PDD-56 and gave an interagency coordination role in SSTR operations to the Office of the Coordinator for Reconstruction and Stability in the U.S. Department of State (commonly referred to by its State Department office symbol, S/CRS).

An interagency office housed at the Department of State and led initially by the Coordinator, Ambassador Carlos Pascual, an experienced Senior Foreign Service Officer and former Ambassador to Ukraine, S/CRS has grown considerably, especially after the publication of NSPD-44. During 2004, S/CRS put together a proposal for

---

[14] For the explanatory paper that accompanied the PDD, see *The Clinton Administrations' Policy on Managing Complex Contingency Operations: Presidential Decision Directive, May 1997.*

how it would structure a capability to field SSTR operations. That proposal included the following planning assumptions:

- the ability to lead two or three SSTR operations concurrently
- a duration of 5 to 10 years for each SSTR operation
- interagency planning that would include the military and civilian elements of government
- a reasonable amount of time for growing and institutionalizing this effort
- that the effort will be able to leverage international resources in most cases.[15]

This interagency-directed concept has been integrated into the NSC decisionmaking system at different levels (see Figure 2.1) and has been articulated in NSPD-44. The principal policy components of that decisionmaking system are NSC Policy Coordinating Committees (PCCs)—the existing regional PCCs and a new PCC for Stability and Reconstruction Operations (SRO PCC)—which provide guidance to S/CRS Country Reconstruction and Stabilization Groups (CRSGs). CRSGs are activated to deal with contingencies. When activated, a CRSG is chaired by the Coordinator, the State Department's regional assistant secretary, and an NSC representative. The CRSG reports to the NSC Deputy's Committee, prepares policy options for the leadership, oversees the S/CRS contribution to country stabilization and reconstruction planning efforts that take place at the Regional Combatant Command headquarters, and oversees field operations.[16]

The S/CRS field components, which could be classified as "planning" and "operational," are the Integration Planning Cells (IPCs), which integrates the CRSG guidelines on post-conflict SSTR operations into military plans drawn up at existing Regional Combatant Commands (RCCs); and the Advance Civilian Team (ACT) Head-

---

[15] State briefing on S/CRS, no date, given to the authors by S/CRS staff in April 2005.

[16] U.S. Department of State, "Office of the Coordinator for Reconstruction and Stabilization (S/CRS)," briefing to RAND project team, no date.

Figure 2.1
U.S. SSTR Response Management

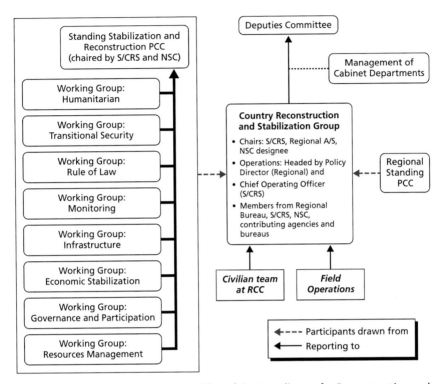

SOURCE: U.S. Department of State, "Office of the Coordinator for Reconstruction and Stabilization (S/CRS)," briefing to RAND project team, no date.
NOTES: A/S = Assistant Secretary; PCC = Policy Coordinating Committee; NSC = National Security Council; RCC = Regional Combatant Commands.
RAND MG580-2.1

quarters, which integrates the operational efforts of Field ACTs that will accompany troops on the ground in the area of concern.[17] The *US Government Draft Planning Framework for Reconstruction, Stabilization, and Conflict Transformation*, prepared jointly by S/CRS and the Joint Forces Command (JFCOM) in December 2005,[18] outlined how the planning and coordination effort might develop. Drawing on earlier

---

[17] ACTs are not replacement for USAID's Disaster Assistance Response Teams (DARTs).

[18] U.S. Joint Forces Command (J7), and U.S. Department of State, Office of the Coordinator for Reconstruction and Stabilization, *US Government Draft Planning Framework for*

research efforts, S/CRS also published the Post-Conflict Reconstruction Essential Tasks Matrix in April 2005,[19] a lengthy list, or menu, of tasks for planners to use in SSTR operations.

S/CRS plans call for a modest-sized core of people to staff the effort:[20]

- 80 diplomats in the Washington-based "core leadership and coordination functions" at S/CRS and staffing the CRSG (of which somewhere between 30 and 40 were on hand at the time of this writing)
- a deployable diplomatic staff of 100 in a proposed Active Response Corps, and a Standing Reserve Corps of 250 to 300 individuals to be built up over five years[21]
- a technical U.S. government Design and Management Skills[22] staff (hereafter the "technical corps") of
  - 30 in Law Enforcement
  - 30 in Rule of Law
  - 90 in Humanitarian, Governance and Economic
- a network of "precompeted" (i.e., prearranged and on-call), standing contracts to provide global coverage in a range of skill sets (numbers not specified)

Reconstruction, Stabilization, and Conflict Transformation, Version 1.0, Washington, D.C., December 2005.

[19] U.S. Department of State, Office of the Coordinator for Reconstruction and Stabilization, *Post-Conflict Reconstruction Essential Tasks*, Washington, D.C., April 2005.

[20] These numbers come from Ambassador Pascual's remarks to the Association of the United States Army, October 4, 2005, and from the S/CRS briefing cited previously. They are illustrative only.

[21] Funding for the reserve corps is subject to congressional legislation. As of the completion of this monograph, the planned number has not been funded.

[22] These numbers come from the S/CRS briefing cited previously and are illustrative only. Interviews with U.S. government officials involved with S/CRS indicate that it has not been able to get a firm commitment from all departments and agencies on manpower, and so these numbers are not indicative of current planning. They do, however, represent at least a preliminary statement of the requirements.

- the possible creation of a "civilian reserve."[23]

The contract personnel would augment these government personnel, who would provide the core staff for and leadership of the effort. To field the contract component, S/CRS plans to maintain an operational database of "skills, contracts, resources and mechanisms throughout the interagency with NGOs, firms, universities, institutes, and think tanks."[24]

The budget needed to support the concept proposed by S/CRS was not supported by the Bush Administration, and appropriations for it have been slow in coming.[25] Of particular importance for this effort, the lion's share of its personnel is envisioned to be supplied by State and USAID. We return to this issue later in Chapters Three and Four, when we discuss the structure of staffs, along with recruiting and retention of personnel for these staffs.

Parallel to the building of civilian infrastructure for SSTR operations, an effort that the Department of Defense has launched aims to alter the way DoD and the armed services approach SSTR operations. Building on the findings of the Defense Science Board 2004 Summer Study, DoD issued Department of Defense Directive 3000.05 (DoDD 3000.05) in November 2005. Explicitly naming stability operations a core mission for the armed forces, the directive mandates that the stability mission be treated with the same level of attention as combat operations.

The services, and particularly the Army, have put together plans to implement DoDD 3000.05. Envisaging much greater cooperation with civilian agencies and civilian personnel, the plans thus rely on the successful implementation of NSPD-44 and the creation of a civilian capacity to implement U.S. policy objectives in SSTR operations. The

---

[23] We are aware of efforts at the Institute for Defense Analyses (IDA) to study *how* a civilian reserve corps could be created. Briefing from, and discussion with, two of the IDA authors, Scott Feil and Martin Lidy, on October 24, 2005.

[24] U.S. Department of State, no date.

[25] Much of the requested money was to establish operational capability, and some of that could be funded out of future supplemental budgets for U.S. response to emergencies.

2006 Quadrennial Defense Review gave clear support to these plans through its reference to the need for unity of effort in SSTR operations across the U.S. government and its explicit acceptance of the National Security Officer Corps, a civilian staff that would be involved in all stages of SSTR operations.[26]

UK Efforts

Notably, the United States was not alone in recognizing shortcomings in fielding a capable civilian staff for SSTR operations. The United Kingdom, too, found it difficult to mobilize the best possible human resources for a SSTR operation, and the steps taken by the UK government largely mirror U.S. actions. The UK approach was to create the Post-Conflict Reconstruction Unit (PCRU) in September 2004, an interagency organization under the MoD, the Foreign and Commonwealth Office (FCO), and the Department for International Development (DFID). DFID controls the budget and operations of the PCRU. The UK government appointed a MoD senior civil servant, Paul Schulte, as director of the PCRU. As the senior UK representative in the CPA ONSA, Schulte had been instrumental in creating the Iraqi Ministry of Defense. The PCRU has taken an approach to mobilizing human resources that is defined by its particular political context and, therefore, is somewhat different from what is likely to develop in the United States.[27] It began by issuing a public announcement soliciting suggestions on how it should structure itself and go about its business. It plans a sparse civilian leadership with private-sector technical experts to provide the majority of the workforce.

Structurally, the PCRU itself is formed into units (economics and finance, security, governance, and social sectors), each of which is responsible for recruiting personnel in its domain. Personnel issues are also likely to be handled somewhat differently than in the United

---

[26] U.S. Department of Defense, *Quadrennial Defense Review Report*, Washington, D.C., February 2006.

[27] The information on the UK approach is from a telephone interview with a senior PCRU Official in December 2004 and from documents shared by the PCRU staff with the study authors.

States. The PCRU is considering six-month tours. The PCRU core staff is to consist of approximately 34 members, whose duties are similar to those of the S/CRS, primarily planning and coordination. The PCRU is developing a standing database of individuals willing to deploy, along with their qualifications.

As organizational changes proceed in the United Kingdom, it may be useful to learn from the UK experience. Since this UK effort has been more resource-constrained than that of the United States, the lessons may be particularly helpful.

CHAPTER THREE

What Capabilities Does the United States Need?

To make recommendations about capabilities that the U.S. government should create, we must first specify the requirements. In Chapter Two, we presented the idea of an A-Team staff and discussed briefly some of the U.S. shortcomings in Iraq in this regard. However, this general articulation of goals is not sufficiently detailed to establish the requirement. In this chapter, we present a framework for considering supply and demand for civilian personnel for staffs in SSTR operations. We begin with the basic question—What is a staff?—and note several other preliminary questions for helping us narrow the scope of the problem.

What Is a Staff?

Had the United States had the right people in Iraq for long enough periods, the situation may have evolved more in line with U.S. goals for that country. However, personnel are only one part of the larger picture of influencing the evolution of that country. Staffs consist not only of people but also of policies, structures, processes, and procedures—in other words, bureaucracies. For any staff to function well, a myriad of questions must be answered: What offices will exist? Who will lead them? To whom will they report and how often? To whom are they accountable? How will bills get paid? Who buys and delivers supplies? What are the procedures for handling classified information? In Iraq, the CPA staff answered many of these and other questions in an *ad hoc* manner, through the efforts of talented and dedicated people. Had those people been deployed into an established and functional organization, the overall effort might have been more effective.

It is also critical to understand that a deployed staff will need to rely heavily on home departments in Washington for support. Such "reachback" capabilities, often used by the military and, increasingly, by U.S. civilian staffs in Iraq and Afghanistan, may play an important part in many future deployments. These practices indicate that a deployed staff needs to be linked with appropriate elements of the U.S. government, such as those elements of Washington agencies that can provide needed support, as well as the NSC staff. Where possible, planners need to lay out these connections, and those individuals that are deployed should have the ability to implement the plans.

A SSTR staff, then, should be made up of an organizational structure, populated by individuals having appropriate skills and experience, and following a set of procedures that permit it to function in the field and leverage capabilities in Washington (and other capitals if it is a multinational effort). We next look at possible sources of staff.

Sources of Staff

Looking at some of the most critical issues raised above—"What offices exist?" "Who is in charge?" "To whom do they report?" and "What are the expected results?"—we can see that the structure, once established, must be led by current or former federal government employees who understand how the government operates and who can effectively link back into the appropriate elements of the government in Washington as needed. Furthermore, recalling our articulation of the A-Team concept, area expertise is needed. This expertise is resident in the U.S. State Department, USAID, some parts of the Defense Department, and the Intelligence Community (IC), and these organizations should be responsible for providing a large portion of that expertise and for managing the effort to gather other needed area experts. Another source of such expertise is private-sector organizations whose personnel regularly work with government foreign-area experts and who understand government's perspectives and structures (e.g., former government employees, and some think tanks and industries).

However, reliance on government experts and systems need not preclude country and area experts from the private sector filling positions in which their particular expertise is helpful (e.g., private-sector development). Furthermore, given the global nature of U.S. interests, we can infer that all regional bureaus of the State Department and USAID, regionally oriented sections of DoD and the IC, and other government agencies with area expertise need to participate in plans for creating an operationally deployable core of specialists. In particular, specific requirements for the personnel systems of those departments and agencies with large numbers of foreign-area experts to supply people with needed skills are outlined in the demands for A-Team personnel.

The S/CRS plan for structuring the SSTR effort is a starting point for considering some of the questions above.

The two policymaking elements of the U.S. government plan for SSTR operations (the S&R PCC and the CRSGs when activated) will be based in and their personnel drawn from the Washington-based staff. The two operational elements (IPCs and ACTs) will be deployed to Regional Combatant Command headquarters (IPC) or into the theater of operations (ACTs). As currently envisioned, they will be staffed from the personnel pool being developed by S/CRS. These government employees, augmented by contract personnel, must be capable of handling two to three SSTR operations simultaneously, each of which may last five to ten years.[1]

The size of the civilian staff will affect what type of personnel systems (e.g., recruiting, retention, management, and contracting) will be needed. Our first observation is that, if SSTR operations are envisioned to be long-term, then the temporal and rotational aspects of staffing SSTR operations should be considered. In particular, the skills needed in the staffs for the first year of a deployment may differ markedly from those of subsequent rotations. If a good progression is made from stabi-

---

[1] We consider the assumption of two or three simultaneous operations reasonable for planning purposes and borne out in the variety of SSTR-like operations undertaken by the United States, or with U.S. participation, in the 1990s (Bosnia-Herzegovina, Kosovo, Macedonia, Haiti, Somalia, and East Timor). That some of the missions were of relatively short duration may have contributed to their lack of success and the reappearance of conditions that led to the interventions in the first place.

lization toward reconstruction over the life of an operation, we would expect the staff composition and size to change with this progression. For example, the first year might require a higher density of experts in mitigating humanitarian crises and reforming the security sector, whereas subsequent years might require more experts in development and governance. In terms of resources and control, the emphasis would also shift from U.S. sources toward those provided by the various international development organizations (e.g., World Bank, United Nations Development Programme [UNDP], NGOs). Some planning must ensure that the skill sets likely to be needed at various stages of SSTR efforts are available. Figure 3.1 presents a notional staffing trajectory. In a nutshell, the overall pattern that could be expected in a successful SSTR operation would be a shift in focus from security and stability to development.

The second observation is that, if U.S. plans envision three deployments at any given time, then, under current S/CRS plans, a small number of U.S. government personnel will be participating in any given effort, and the United States will have a large percentage of

Figure 3.1
Hypothetical Staffing Profile

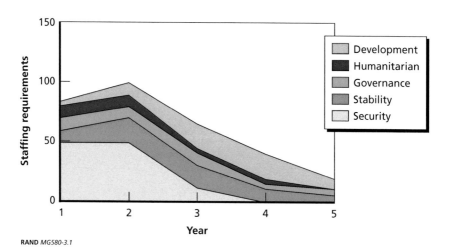

its deployable government personnel participating in ongoing SSTR operations at any given time. Table 3.1 lays out notionally how many U.S. government personnel could be deployed on a given operation under different assumptions of the sizes of the deployable staff.

For all cases, we have assumed that the United States will be involved in three simultaneous operations. The columns of the table correspond to the frequency of individual deployments and identify the number of personnel deployed per operation. The first column corresponds to a requirement for SSTR personnel to deploy one out of every three years, and the second for personnel to deploy one out of every five years. The rows correspond to different assumptions about the composition and usage of reserves. Row 1 assumes that the U.S. government will not use reserves on routine deployments, and so does not count them as available for deployment. Row 2 assumes that a diplomatic reserve will be deployed as frequently as the active diplomatic corps, and Row 3 assumes that there will be a technical corps reserve of 450 personnel (the same ratio of active to reserve members as for the diplomatic corps plan), and that these personnel will deploy as needed.

Table 3.1
Number of U.S. Government Personnel Deployed per Operation Under S/CRS Staffing Assumptions

		Personnel per Deployment	
Composition and Usage		**Deployed One of Three Years**	**Deployed One of Five Years**
1	Active diplomatic and technical corps (250)	28	17
2	Active diplomatic and active technical corps plus reserve diplomatic corps (500 to 550)	62	37
3	Active and reserve diplomatic and technical corps (1,000)	112	67
4	Active diplomatic and technical corps deployed all the time (250)	84	84

Row 4 assumes that the United States deploys all diplomatic corps personnel constantly, and that the reserve is a base from which personnel rotate into and out of the active corps each year. Hence, the number is constant across this row. The numbers in the table represent the total U.S. government personnel on each deployment. One can arrive at the numbers by dividing the total number of available U.S. government personnel (according to the assumptions above) by the number of simultaneous operations (three, by the criteria articulated by S/CRS) and the frequency of deployment. For example, given a total of 250 active diplomatic and technical corps members, and assuming that each member will be deployed one out of every three years (that is, one-third of the personnel is available to deploy at a given time) and that three deployments are ongoing at any given time, we have:

$$250/(3 \times 3) = 27.8 \text{ personnel per operation.}$$

This is the number, rounded up to 28, in the top left cell of Table 3.1.[2]

The personnel totals presented in Table 3.1 do not represent a large contingent for any operation, although some of the cases might be sufficient if the United States were participating in a multinational effort in a small country. Furthermore, they do not count contract personnel, large numbers of whom might be needed (we examine the ratio of government to contract personnel in the CPA in a subsequent section).

Furthermore, a unilateral SSTR effort in a mid-sized country would likely require deploying the total envisioned U.S. government personnel in the active and reserve diplomatic corps and the technical corps, even if augmented with a significant number of contract personnel. Additionally, we note that, if the cadre of deployable U.S.

---

[2]   Also assumed in these numbers is that these deployments are to austere and dangerous places, which leads to the need for rotation. As noted, these numbers include both diplomatic and technical corps personnel. This is an important distinction, because Foreign Service Officers are used to spending a large part of their career overseas, although not in austere and dangerous situations, whereas technical corps personnel would not have such expectations.

government personnel includes area experts for different parts of the world, then, unless area experts for all areas were to be deployed to the mid-sized country in question, the number available for a given effort would be considerably smaller because experts in one area of the world would not be available to deploy to other areas. Again, we investigate the implications of area skills in a subsequent section.

Further complicating the equation, the small number of U.S. government personnel available to deploy at any given time and the assumption that U.S. government personnel will be the leaders of SSTR efforts imply that almost all government personnel will be leaders and, therefore, should be relatively senior in grade. This implication raises the question of how to develop relatively senior people over their careers if there are no or relatively few junior positions for civil servants or Foreign Service Officers (FSOs). Looking then at the requirements of the proposed structure of having an IPC, an ACT Headquarters, and several Field ACTs performing planning and operational functions for each deployment, we conclude that the problems in creating a pool of appropriate civilian staff for SSTR operations seem difficult to overcome without substantially larger personnel commitments.

Finally, we note that, unless SSTR operations take place in countries with an existing and well-staffed U.S. Embassy or the Combatant Commander remains in charge for the duration of the SSTR effort, then insurmountable problems will exist, because S/CRS plans make no provisions for staffing a new structure to provide the overall leadership for an effort (as the United States did in Iraq).

At the next level of detail, efficient staffs are not simply people recruited when needed and sent overseas to fill empty positions; rather, they are groups of professionals who understand their organization and its mission, and, if possible, have had the opportunity to develop working relationships. Optimally, this last requirement would be met by people who have worked together prior to deploying or, minimally, by people who have worked in the same organization (if one exists, which it currently does not) and are familiar with the way things are done.

In addition, there are several ways to categorize billets in a staff and to propose required skills for, or characteristics of, the people who fill them. Focusing on those characteristics specifically useful for SSTR operations, we find that the major categories (which are binary according to whether a billet is coded to indicate a needed characteristic or a person who has that characteristic), besides subject-matter expertise and experience, include such items as

- area expertise
- language skills
- U.S. citizenship
- U.S. government employee
- security clearance.

Consideration of all the above factors leads us to believe that HR management (deciding on staffing needs, recruiting and training, ensuring high performance, managing benefits and compensation, keeping accurate records, and establishing appropriate policies) is an essential element of the success of any SSTR operation.

The A-Team Concept, Revisited

Having considered requirements and staffing sources, we shift focus back to the concept of an A-Team to expound on its elements from the perspective of assessing the critical aspects of staffing a long-term effort such as a SSTR operation.

Continuity. Staff members should deploy for at least one year. Every U.S. official interviewed for this study who addressed this issue indicated that the processes for establishing relationships and building trust with indigenous officials, supplying the continuity needed for establishing and running offices and programs, and simply ensuring that excessive time is not spent in transition (or worse, having no transition) require that staff members remain in country for a minimum of one year. Some interviewees believed that one year was not sufficient, citing the U.S. experience in Vietnam, where, in the words of Colonel John Paul Vann, "We don't have twelve years' experience in Vietnam. We have one year's experience twelve times over. . . ."[3]

---

[3]   Quoted in D. Michael Shafer, *The Legacy: The Vietnam War in the American Imagination*, Boston, Mass.: Beacon Press, 1990, p. 100.

The Iraq experience demonstrates the damage done when people in positions that require developing relationships and trust with Iraqi leaders, or responsibility for important policies or programs, left before fulfilling their tasks. This requirement is not without controversy or difficulty. As mentioned in Chapter Two, the emerging UK policy is to have six-month rotations, based on the assumption that people burn out rapidly in austere and stressful environments. Furthermore, releasing valuable employees for detail to another agency or operation for long periods poses difficulties for the agencies giving up these people, whose staffs may already be stretched thin. Also, finding civilians willing to go for more than six months to austere areas in which the risk of violence is often real may be difficult. However, the operational requirement universally articulated by U.S. personnel who have been involved in these types of operations clearly indicates that the goal should be year-long tours.

Professional and Technical Expertise. Staffs run well only when each individual has the expertise to work without significant on-the-job training—a factor made all the more important by the transient nature of the staffs. SSTR staffs are the same as any other staff with regard to requirements for competency and experience. These requirements are particularly important at the beginning of a SSTR effort when time is critical. Indigenous populations may have unrealistically high expectations, and violence can easily flourish when there is little visible progress. The words of a senior Shia militia leader make such expectations abundantly clear regarding the U.S. occupation of Iraq: "If you could defeat Saddam's army in three weeks [sic], surely you could rebuild the country in three months, and that's what we expected."[4]

In Iraq, it was not unusual for CPA staff to work in areas for which they were not qualified by training. As cited earlier, missile-defense experts worked on personnel and training issues for the Ministry of Defense. In another instance, an expert in Demilitarization, Demobilization and Reintegration (DDR) of former combatants worked instead on anti-corruption efforts.[5]

---

[4] Stated in a meeting with Kelly in Baghdad during April 2004.

[5] Kelly's observations, based on experience in Iraq.

Experience Level. Similar to professional and technical-area qualifications, experience level is critical to making proper recommendations to senior policymakers and performing staff functions without much oversight—critical in fast-moving, fluid situations encountered in SSTR operations. Again, based on the authors' observations, there were many inexperienced people either in senior positions or acting as advisors on key topics to senior policymakers at the CPA in Baghdad. While dedicated and capable, they simply did not have the experience to understand the situations they faced or the skill to make things happen. Additionally, in many cultures (such as those in the Middle East), age, seniority, and gender indicate gravitas and importance. Young, inexperienced people in senior jobs are not taken seriously or, worse, are perceived as showing a lack of seriousness on the part of the United States. While cultural sensitivities need not dictate U.S. staffing procedures, the staffing choices have consequences that policymakers need to consider.

Area Expertise. Not everyone on a SSTR staff needs to be an expert in the area of the world in which the SSTR operation is taking place, but those in key positions should be, or should be advised by people with these skills. Without area experts, it is difficult to safely and successfully operate, and to make the kind of decisions needed for success. The ability to work well with the indigenous leadership is, in some cases, fleeting and can deteriorate quickly if things are not carried out well from the start. Having area expertise in key advisory, policy-making, and operational billets is essential.

However, not all staff members need to be area experts. Requiring area experts for too many billets reduces the population of people who can fill them, thus creating potential recruiting problems for the first and subsequent rotations.[6] Furthermore, for a country such as the United States, which has global-security and humanitarian interests, the number of area experts required to fill all areas of interest

---

[6]   In a well-planned operation, personnel identified for deployment on subsequent rotations may have time to train sufficiently to develop a reasonable level of expertise (e.g., cultural and historical studies, familiarizing themselves with relevant issues). Those on a first or second rotation would almost surely not have time to develop language skills from scratch, unless enrolled in an immersion program.

in the world would quickly rise to unreasonable levels. On the other hand, the pool of those who are qualified in the first three categories of A-Team traits (see p. 12) can be used on deployments to any area of the world, whereas those filling billets requiring area expertise are more limited.

Working in Austere and Dangerous Locations. By definition, SSTR operations take place in areas in which security is not yet established. If the past is any guide, most SSTR operations will take place in developing countries, which have poor infrastructures that are sometimes made worse by strife. Any civilian deploying to such an area must understand the inherent dangers and be willing to accept them as part of the job.

What Staffs Are Needed?

The following three questions, along with what they imply for needed U.S. capability, are a first step to addressing staffing needs:

- Will the United States act unilaterally or in *ad hoc* coalitions, or will it act as part of a standing multinational organization?
- What is the time horizon for SSTR efforts?
- Will the United States plan to execute SSTR operations worldwide or focus on specific areas of interest?

Planners must address each of these questions, as well as what is practical given constraints on personnel and resources. We address each of these questions in turn here.

Unilateral or Multilateral Effort?

The answer to this question will depend on a given administration's views of the stakes of the mission and its inclinations to involve partners. However, the creation of institutional capacity cannot be dependent on such transient factors, since building and maintaining the capabilities and capacity to conduct unilateral SSTR missions take time and resources. If experience is any guide, the United States should expect to have coalition partners who would contribute some talent and resources. Therefore, the issue essentially reduces itself to whether the United States should plan to provide the overall structure and leadership for an effort, such as in Iraq, or just components of a multilateral effort, such as in Kosovo, where the United States was one among many participants and a variety of countries and international organizations (UN, European Union [EU], Organization for Security and Cooperation in Europe [OSCE], North Atlantic Treaty Organization [NATO]) that contributed to the SSTR operation. Having the capacity to field the overall leadership structure does not mean that the United States will act unilaterally or even that planning for multilateral efforts should not be the primary concern. In our judgment, the U.S. political leadership should retain the option to act unilaterally, even if policy indicates that planning and preparation will be for multilateral efforts.

Related to the unilateral-multilateral issue is the question, "What should the United States plan to do in concert with other states that are likely to be partners in future SSTR operations?" In particular, different allies have different areas of national competence. The United States, for example, does not maintain national health or education systems, so countries that do have such systems might be better suited than the United States to lead the health and education components of a coalition effort. Expertise in such realms may exist in the United States, although not necessarily in the federal government, or in the federal departments or agencies that might be expected to lead such efforts. For example, the Veterans Administration runs a nationwide health system, so it might play a lead role if no coalition partner was available, and large-city governments could supply significant expertise in running large school systems. On the other hand, some areas, such as military forces or financial and business sectors, are areas in which U.S. federal expertise could be brought to bear.

Finally, the federal government is not the sole repository of expertise. State and local governments, the private sector, and allies have expertise that can be planned for when developing and prioritizing the standing organizational structures that must be in place if SSTR operations are to hit the ground running. For example, it might make sense

to have standing arrangements made for federal, state, and local government staff; allies; and private-sector contributions for the delivery
of certain services, and to have backup capabilities in all areas ready for
deployment. S/CRS may be moving in that direction with its plan for a
Standby Response Corps and the Global Skills Network (precompeted
standing contracts).

Time Horizon for SSTR Efforts?

The Planning Framework for SSTR operations indicates a long-
term time horizon, with short-term goals referred to as being in the
2–3-year time frame.[7] Other planning guidance from S/CRS indicates
a time frame for U.S. involvement of five to ten years.[8] This duration
implies establishing staggered rotational schedules so that continuity
in staff longevity is maintained. Preferably a number of staff members
would be required to stay for longer than a year on the first rotation;
alternately, some could be required to leave early so that appropriate
overlap and rotation could be instituted and maintained. The requirements for the initial staff period of a SSTR effort will likely be different
at the later periods.

Second and subsequent rotations of staff personnel need not be
maintained on the same level of readiness as the initial group. During
the year leading up to the second group of staff's deploying to theater
(or more for subsequent rotations), there is time to recruit and train
staff members. Furthermore, greater flexibility may be needed in preparing for the second and subsequent rotations, because the situation
in the host country in the second and subsequent years will not be
known immediately, and different skills will likely be needed.

**Plan to Execute SSTR Operations Worldwide or Focus on Specific
Areas of Interest?**

This question goes directly to the size of the effort needed by the U.S.
government. S/CRS guidance indicates that the United States envisions

---

[7]   U.S. Joint Forces Command (J7), U.S. Department of State, Office of the Coordinator
for Reconstruction and Stabilization (2005), p. 21.

[8]   S/CRS briefing charts provided to Kelly, 2005.

participating in up to three concurrent operations, but the assumption calls into question the size of each operation, noting that S/CRS plans are for small deployments focused on providing assistance and coordination, rather than on standing up a full-fledged occupational government and providing large-scale assistance, as in the effort in Iraq.

To understand the requirements, we look at a scenario for deployment that puts maximal stress on the personnel system. The S/CRS guidance to prepare for three concurrent SSTR operations, each lasting five to ten years, could result in all three being in one general area (e.g., the Middle East, Africa, or Latin America). If so, the entities within the federal government would be required to have area experts, from whatever source, trained and ready to deploy at three times the numbers needed for any one operation, and to have plans in place to provide replacements. If each geographic area, bureaucratically thought of in terms of government organizations (e.g., geographic bureaus at the State Department), must prepare for this scenario, then the demands on the U.S. government and its partners in all other sources of supply are large. This may be a reasonable assumption for some areas and not for others.

Returning to the original question of what staffs are needed, we estimate that the effort required to create the capability to field three simultaneous, CPA-sized staffs (the worst-case situation) would entail resources that, at this time, make the creation of such a capability prohibitively costly. That said, the S/CRS plan for approximately 500 to 600 government staff (active and reserve) augmented by a yet-to-be-determined number of contractors may be insufficient (essentially, the best-case situation).

Without firm policy for guidance, we are left to postulate a mid-case set of requirements to continue this analysis. Taking into account the need for three simultaneous efforts, we use as a point of reference a deployable staff the size of the CPA to cover all three SSTR operations, and use 3,000 as an approximate number of civilian personnel (government and contractor) deployed at any given time to fill that requirement.[9] The 3,000 civilian personnel could include both active and reserve elements.[10]

First, if we use the ratio of diplomatic to technical staff contained in the S/CRS staffing proposals,[11] approximately 40 percent of the deployed U.S. government staff would serve in diplomatic roles and 60 percent in "technical" roles. We turn next to identifying the ratio of contractor to U.S. government staff. We did not find a fixed staffing document that differentiates government from private-sector billets; therefore, exact numbers for these two portions of the staff cannot be given with certainty. However, if we use the ratios present in the CPA at the time of the Personnel Assessment Team's report to the Secretary of Defense, approximately one-third of deployed personnel were contractors.[12] Using these ratios, we can conclude a need for approximately 800 government diplomats, 1,200 government technical staff, and 1,000 contract personnel.[13] These could be active or reserve person-

---

[9] There was never a firm organizational table for Iraq, so this number is based on estimates. The February Report to the Secretary of Defense, U.S. Department of Defense, *Personnel Assessment Team Report to the Secretary of Defense*, Washington, D.C., February 2004, indicated that there were 1,856 authorized slots (p. 7), but also that there were 474 positions about to be added to the authorization. Elsewhere (p. 8), the same document stated that Ambassador Bremer's staff consisted of 2,693 authorized slots. Estimates range from slightly under 2,000 to about 3,000. We will use 3,000 as a working figure. Our assumption disregards the fact that some of the CPA staff was military.

[10] We note that our hypothetical 3,000-person requirement was not produced by analysis of needs; rather, it is presented as a number that seems reasonable to us, and it serves as a starting point for analysis. Should the actual requirement be different, the calculations could be replicated with the agreed-upon requirement as a starting point.

[11] There is no formal requirement for technical corps personnel. According to an interview with one former S/CRS staffer, the original proposal was for 132 technical billets, whereas an early number used for illustrative purposes by S/CRS was 150. For just the ratios of active corps personnel, we will assume approximately 40 percent diplomatic corps and 60 percent technical corps (of the government staff) for purposes of this analysis. We further assume that the reserve corps ratios will be the same.

[12] According to the Personnel Assessment Team's report (U.S. Department of Defense, 2004, p. 7), 666 contractors were on the CPA staff in Iraq out of 1,856 authorized personnel. The total authorized number was to increase before the end of the CPA.

[13] Note that these contract personnel do not include logistics, maintenance, and support contractors. They are people filling staff positions.

nel, where reserve personnel could be drawn from the ranks of retired government officials. We note as well from the CPA experience that a large number of the government employees were temporary, brought on under the authority of U.S. Code, Title 5, Section 3161 (referred to as "3161s").

Second, note that it is not a requirement to have a standing staff of 3,000 but, rather, a requirement to be able to deploy such a staff when needed. In particular, area experts for all areas of concern for the United States must be trained and ready to deploy. Exactly what this number would be is not knowable without creating a manning table for the proposed organizations. However, if we assume that 10 percent of the 2,000 government staff must be area experts, the U.S. government must be prepared to deploy 200 area experts. Referring back to the earlier discussion about the need to deploy up to three simultaneous SSTR operations in any given area and using the number of State Department regional bureaus as a guide,[14] the number of area experts needed will be six times higher than those who would actually be deployed. Therefore, 1,800 generalists (i.e., those without area expertise) and 1,200 area experts (200 in each of the six areas associated with State Department regional bureaus) would be required to be deployable, for a total requirement of 3,000 federal government personnel, not including contract personnel on the staff.

The above discussion describes the assumptions and functional requirement for the number and general type of personnel the United States must be prepared to deploy. Reserve corps personnel in the S/CRS rubric are not included in this number, although our discussion of the A-Team concept describes the general characteristics of such staffs. Together, these two categories represent the demand for personnel for the large civilian staffs for SSTR operations. We have also described above the supply sources of personnel. The two sides of the question are depicted in Figure 3.2.

---

[14] There are six State Department regional bureaus: African Affairs, Near East Asian Affairs, South Asian Affairs, East Asian and Pacific Affairs, European and Eurasian Affairs, and Western Hemisphere Affairs.

Figure 3.2
Supply of and Demand for Personnel

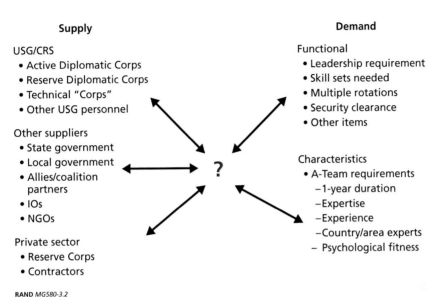

Supply

USG/CRS
- Active Diplomatic Corps
- Reserve Diplomatic Corps
- Technical "Corps"
- Other USG personnel

Other suppliers
- State government
- Local government
- Allies/coalition partners
- IOs
- NGOs

Private sector
- Reserve Corps
- Contractors

Demand

Functional
- Leadership requirement
- Skill sets needed
- Multiple rotations
- Security clearance
- Other items

Characteristics
- A-Team requirements
  - 1-year duration
  - Expertise
  - Experience
  - Country/area experts
  - Psychological fitness

?

RAND MG580-3.2

Note that the sources of supply and demand are fairly well defined. What is missing is the machinery to connect the two, represented by the question mark in the center of the figure. In Chapter Four, we discuss this element and in the final chapter put forth options and recommendations on how to fill this need.

Process, Structure, and Management—What Can Be Done Today?

In Chapters One through Three, we described the purpose for this research, gave a brief overview of the approaches being taken by the United States and the United Kingdom to create the capability to staff SSTR efforts, and presented a framework for considering supply and demand for personnel. We begin this chapter with an overview of the bureaucratic, statutory, and regulatory machinery and processes that are currently in place and that could be used to create such a capability. We then turn to structure and management considerations.

Our interviewees acknowledged that the United States did not send the A-Team to Iraq. Neither the structure for such a staff nor the ability to recruit and deploy the necessary personnel quickly was in place. Our assessment in Chapter Three shows that current S/CRS plans would not be sufficient should the United States need to deploy even a moderate-sized operational capability to more than one location at a time. However, the fact that the United States did not field a competent staff in Iraq does not necessarily mean that the U.S. government would not have had the capability to field a competent staff had it been prepared for this mission and had there been structures and processes in place to demand and supply such a staff. That is, it does not mean that the human-resources systems of the U.S. government as they currently exist could not have supplied the required personnel, had they been appropriately tasked to do so.

By looking at existing authorities and changes in management and leadership that could help remedy these shortfalls, in this chapter we identify what could be done today if the U.S. government were organized and prepared to fill these requirements without any changes to regulation or law.

Existing Authorities

The paradox of using federal civilians in reconstruction and stabilization efforts is that, generally, federal civilians move out of, rather than into, areas of political instability. A complete playbook for identifying, obtaining, and organizing human resources for deployment to an unstable area simply does not exist. There are, however, statutes, rules, and policies that provided the foundation upon which federal civilians served in Iraq and could serve in the future in other SSTR operations. One of the most difficult bureaucratic tasks facing CPA and other U.S. government agencies was recruiting employees and other individuals interested in and available for assignment to Iraq. Without changes, the same problem is likely to reappear in future contingencies. In general, once identified, candidates must be assessed with regard to qualifications and suitability, appointed, then compensated and managed. We discuss each of these tasks below.

Identifying Detailees

According to the GAO, approximately 26 percent of the CPA staff was detailed from DoD and other federal agencies. Most were volunteers, even though there are a number of authorities that may provide for the involuntary assignment of civilians to SSTR areas. U.S. government civilian personnel were not deployed involuntarily in any significant number.

Not all U.S. government departments and agencies have the same defined authorities. Foreign Service Officers can be involuntarily assigned overseas, although this has not happened in large numbers since Vietnam, and they can resign rather than accept such an assignment. Moreover, the population of FSOs available for such assignments is relatively small. For example, the largest foreign service is the State

Department's,[1] consisting of 11,238 officers as of December 2005.[2] At that time, 7,431 were stationed at overseas posts (e.g., embassies and consulates). In addition to FSOs, there are also approximately 8,000 civil service employees at the Department of State, of which only eight were assigned overseas, as well as foreign nationals that the Department hires at its overseas posts. USAID's foreign service is approximately one-tenth the size.

Department of Defense civilians can be assigned to positions that support long-term and short-term emergencies and combat operations. For positions that support combat operations, the authority is position-based, according to United States Code, Title 10, Section 1580, which grants the Secretary of Defense authority to designate as "Emergency-Essential" any DoD employee whose position has the following attributes:

- Provides immediate and continuing support for combat operations or to support maintenance and repair of combat-essential systems of the armed forces.
- Must be performed in a combat zone after the evacuation of non-essential personnel from the zone in connection with a war, a national emergency declared by Congress or the President, or the commencement of combat operations of the armed forces in the zone.
- Is unsuitable for conversion to military because of the necessity for duty to be performed without interruption.

The number of emergency-essential positions is relatively small, and questions remain regarding the authority of DoD to assign a civilian not in an emergency-essential position involuntarily to a combat area or hardship tour, such as on a SSTR operation. Some in the DoD HR community believe the Department has the authority to assign

---

[1] The U.S. Agency for International Development and the Departments of Agriculture and Commerce have foreign services also, although significantly smaller than the State Department's.

[2] Phone conversation with a representative of the State Department's Resource Management Organization Analysis (RMOA) office.

personnel overseas to SSTR operations involuntarily; however, not everyone agrees, and as a matter of law, this issue is not settled.[3]

While non-DoD agencies have no similar authority, expertise from these departments (e.g., Health, Education, Transportation, Energy) is needed in SSTR operations. A brief review of how some HR functions were handled for the CPA illustrates several key points regarding recruiting, assessing, appointing, and compensating individuals for work in Iraq.

Recruiting New Hires

Volunteers were solicited using a number of formal and informal mechanisms. Formal methods included a DoD Web site, at which interested individuals could submit applications; a DoD contract with a minority company to identify Arabic-speaking U.S. citizens willing to serve; and, later, the use of traditional vacancy announcements and standard DoD recruiting tools and Web sites. Perhaps the most effective tool in the early days was personal contact, whereby senior DoD and administration officials went directly to individuals known to have the skills, aptitude, and willingness to serve and solicited applications.

Unfortunately, in some cases, once a volunteer was identified, mid-level managers charged with running offices with small staffs were hesitant, if not outright resistant, to allow the volunteer to deploy because it would have impaired the functioning of their offices.[4] Bureaucratically, this is understandable: Managers generally could not hire replacements for deploying employees. The affected offices had to work short-handed until the deployed employee returned while absorbing the cost of the employee's pay and benefits—often incremented significantly because of danger pay, overtime, and other compensation earned while assigned to the CPA. We also understand that some federal employees were reluctant to apply for temporary positions in Iraq because policies regarding the authority for them to return to their permanent jobs, as well as their consideration while away for such things as promotions and performance awards, were unclear.

---

[3]   Interview with a senior Army personnel manager, July 6, 2005.

[4]   Personal experience, Tunstall.

Assessing Detailees

Regardless of how an individual is recruited, once that individual is identified, it is critical to assess his or her qualifications and suitability to perform the job. Because most CPA employees were appointed using the provisions of United States Code, Title 5, Section 3161 (5 USC 3161), which will be discussed later in this section (e.g., in Appointing Employees), the standard rules for assessing, rating, and ranking applicants did not apply and were not used extensively in the early days. The CPA staff and others conducted extensive interviews and vetted all applicants; however, because the mission evolved and changed quickly, descriptions of duties to be performed were general rather than detailed. Whether for outside applicants or detailees, the descriptions often did not identify specific qualifications or requirements against which one could accurately measure the capability of a job applicant or the applicant's likelihood for success in a highly charged, fast-paced, and insecure environment. It follows then, that the assessment was not always well linked to the job requirements.

In addition, consideration of the candidate's suitability for the position and ability to obtain a security clearance is an important element of assessment. The delay in receiving security clearances deterred some individuals: They could not deploy until the clearance was received, so the organization was harmed because the clearance-process time delayed the arrival of needed personnel. We understand that OPM and DoD are working to improve clearance processing; if resolved, such delays might not be a factor in future SSTR efforts.

Appointing Employees

The single most important tool in hiring civilians for Iraq was the authority provided by 5 USC 3161, which gives wide latitude to appoint and compensate employees to staff a temporary organization that has been established by law or Executive Order. Because the CPA, as well as its predecessor and successor organizations, was established by Executive Order, the 3161 provisions were available to DoD and, later, to the Department of State. At the CPA, the "3161s" hired under this authority occupied critical positions—in many cases, the most senior positions in the CPA. Many were identified using nontraditional methods, such as direct solicitations from senior government officials, and were often paid at rates generally above those received by individuals with similar experience who occupy General Schedule positions elsewhere in the government, including the detailees discussed earlier.

This method of hiring personnel has some important drawbacks. First, the 3161 hiring authority places the burden of hiring all types of personnel on the human-resources department of the lead agency—the DoD for the CPA. As a result, the U.S. government organization most capable of finding qualified people was often not used. For example, to find a health advisor, the considerable capabilities of the Department of Health and Human Services may not have been used to the fullest. Of particular importance for long-term SSTR efforts, personnel hired under this authority ("3161s"), since they are temporary employees, generally do not stay in the government when their term of service expires, so the expertise developed during their time overseas is lost to the federal government.

Other available, although little used, appointment tools were the direct-hire authority that OPM granted to fill positions critical to the reconstruction efforts, and the use of the Intergovernmental Personnel Act (IPA) mobility program to bring in personnel from think tanks, universities, and state and local governments. Using direct hire, a relatively new authority, any U.S. government agency could, with OPM approval, quickly fill positions without regard to usual merit staffing requirements.

Compensating Employees

The U.S. government's failure to establish a consistent set of compensation and benefit packages for all civilian personnel working for the federal government at the CPA was a source of friction and a potential source of suboptimal performance. Pay rates for most federal civilians are established by the OPM under Chapter 53 of Title 5, United States Code. OPM is also responsible for most rules and regulations that govern premium pay, including overtime. However, because of differences in pay systems and the latitude available to agencies in applying the rules, employees working side by side sometimes received different compensation. For example, a member of the Senior Executive Service detailed from a Defense activity to the CPA worked beside a 3161 whose basic pay rate was equal to the SES member's pay rate. Both worked the long hours typical for CPA employees. However, the 3161 received overtime pay and the SES did not, because employees in the Senior Executive Service are not eligible for overtime.

The CPA generally did not use recruitment, relocation, and retention incentives provided by the Federal Workplace Flexibility Act of 2004—up to 25 percent of the employee's basic pay, or, with OPM approval, up to 50 percent—but they could be effective tools for future SSTR efforts. An agency may pay a recruitment incentive to a newly appointed employee if the agency determines that the position is likely to be difficult to fill in the absence of an incentive. An agency may pay a relocation incentive to a current employee who must relocate to accept a position in a different geographic location, again if the agency determines that the position is likely to be difficult to fill in the absence of an incentive. An agency may pay a retention incentive if it determines that the unusually high or unique qualifications of the employee or a special need of the agency for the employee's services makes it essential to retain the employee and that the employee would be likely to leave the federal service in the absence of the incentive. The incentives may be given as an initial lump-sum payment at the beginning of a service period, in installments throughout a service period, as a final lump-sum payment upon completion of the service period, or in a combination of these methods.

The Workforce Flexibility Act also modified the critical-pay authority under which OPM may, upon the request of an agency head and after consultation with OMB, grant authority to fix the rate of basic pay for one or more critical positions up to the rate for Level I of the Executive Schedule ($180,100 in 2005). Under this same provision of law, a higher rate of pay may be established upon the President's written approval. In order to apply the critical-pay authority to a position, the position must require a very high level of expertise in a scientific, technical, professional, or administrative field and be crucial to the accomplishment of an agency's mission. This authority, while not used in Iraq, could be useful in the future.

Similar to the issues related to differing application of compensation policies discussed above, whereby the General Services Administration's Federal Travel Regulations and the Department of State's Standardized Regulations appropriately give agencies latitude in applying the regulations, differences in entitlements and compensation for similarly situated employees can occur. Many detailees traveled to Iraq on temporary-duty travel orders and were never officially detailed to the CPA. The employee's home organization paid the employee's salary and additional compensation, such as eminent-danger pay, foreign post differential, and overtime. Increased compensation expenses, coupled with mission requirements that did not change just because an employee was away on detail, reduced the U.S. government's enthusiasm to provide volunteers.

Different agencies also had different policies for leave, especially home and administrative leave. State Department employees had more leave flexibility during the CPA period than did DoD civilian employees, 3161s, or those on IPA assignments—another potential source of friction and discontent. However, there is also an argument that greater flexibility in incentives is needed to recruit the best people from the public or private sectors.[5] We discuss this need in greater detail in Chapter Five.

Training, Deployment, and Redeployment

By the time the Department of State assumed responsibility in Baghdad, deployment processing had evolved to an efficient and effective system, although the evolution was not without angst. Civilian and military personnel generally entered Iraq through a central processing center in Kuwait, using DoD's Common Access Card (CAC) and a copy of the official travel orders to enter the country without visas. Deploying civilians processed through military deployment centers in either Virginia or Texas, but they received little in the way of country orientation. As organizational responsibility transferred from DoD to

---

[5]   We use the term *public sector* to refer to government at the federal, state, and local levels. When we are referring only to the federal government, we use the term *U.S. government* or *federal government*.

State, the Department of State implemented a formal predeployment training and information program that included country orientation.

Throughout the life of the CPA, redeployment remained an issue. Tours of duty for civilians were flexible. The 3161 employees, primarily because they were temporary, could resign or rotate on a whim. There was no official process for handing off job assignments or sharing procedures, processes, or insights. These shortcomings could have been alleviated with a more effective structure and management controls typically used by established organizations.

There are some authorities that could be helpful but that currently are not in place. First, the United States has historically fielded law enforcement officers to SSTR operations through civilian contractors. Police officers who wish to participate in SSTR operations usually have to leave their home departments to sign up with the federal contractor, and they have no guarantee that they will be able to return to their home department when they are done. A statute such as the one that protects the jobs and status of military reservists who are called up could be helpful in recruiting law enforcement professionals for SSTR duties.[6]

Additionally, pay and incentive rules that prevent some employees from getting the full benefits of additional remuneration typically provided in dangerous operations and overtime pay deserve to be examined and perhaps modified. For example, the statute that caps the pay for federal employees at the level of an Executive Level 1 salary could be waived so that mid- and senior-level personnel could receive the full percentage of hazardous-duty differential pay offered to other employees.

Summary of Existing Authorities

Table 4.1 summarizes the authorities discussed in this monograph. It is not all-inclusive with regard to federal hiring and compensation.

---

[6] For a discussion of the problem of, and potential solutions for, providing professional transitional law enforcement capabilities for SSTR operations, see Terrence K. Kelly, *Options for Transitional Security Capabilities for America*, Santa Monica, Calif.: RAND Corporation, TR-353-A, 2006.

Rather, readers should refer to OPM (www.opm.gov) and agency Web sites for detailed information.

All of these authorities could have been used in Iraq. That they were not used or were used differently by different agencies with differing results suggests that flexibility in the absence of a comprehensive planning model may not be the solution. For this reason, we present a framework for such a model in the next section.

Human Capital Assessment and Accountability Framework

As part of the President's Management Agenda, OPM is leading the federal government's Strategic Management of Human Capital Initiative and has developed a comprehensive model—the Human Capital Assessment and Accountability Framework—that federal

Table 4.1
Summary of Authorities

Flexibility	Authorizing Statute/Regulation
Emergency-Essential assignment of DoD employees to positions supporting long- and short-term emergencies and combat operations	10 USC 1580
Hiring employees for temporary organizations that are established by law or Executive Order	5 USC 3161
Intergovernmental Personnel Act mobility program	5 USC 3371–3375, 5 CFR part 334
Direct Hire	5 USC 3304, 5 CFR 337 subpart B
Recruitment Incentive	5 USC 5753, 5 CFR part 575, subpart A
Relocation Incentive	5 USC 5753, 5 CFR part 575, subpart B
Retention Incentive	5 USC 5754, 5 CFR part 575, subpart C
Critical Pay	Federal Workforce Flexibility Act of 2004, Section 102

NOTE: CFR = Code of Federal Regulations.

agencies must use in developing human-resources programs.[7] The Framework, described on OPM's Web site, provides a guide to those issues deserving of most consideration by those creating the capability to field large civilian staffs. The Framework includes critical success factors and metrics for SSTR planners, and we use it to assess the elements of a system to provide civilian staffs in SSTR operations. Had a process based on this model been in place and used to plan and staff the CPA, then a more appropriate staff, perhaps even one resembling an A-Team, might have been fielded for the CPA.

The Framework advocates the following:

- strategic alignment, including workforce planning and deployment
- leadership and knowledge management
- results-oriented performance culture
- talent management
- accountability.

We examine each of these characteristics below, focusing on strategic alignment and talent management, those parts of the Framework that are most relevant to SSTR planning and execution.

Strategic Alignment

OPM describes *strategic alignment* as a system "that promotes alignment of human capital management strategies with agency mission, goals, and objectives through analysis, planning, investment, measurement and management of human capital programs." Strategic alignment requires that an agency describe human-capital goals that support mission accomplishment, set progress milestones, identify those responsible for the milestones, and include human-capital activities in

---

[7] We use the Human Capital Assessment and Accountability Framework because it is a validated existing tool mandated for use by U.S. government agencies. Our assessment is a preliminary one, derived from discussions of the research team and based on subject-matter expertise. The evaluation criteria and associated metrics deserve additional attention. We encourage and welcome work that would extend this effort further.

annual budget requests. For our purposes, in addition to planning and resources, a critical component of creating a well-functioning personnel system aligned with the strategic goals of the U.S. SSTR operation is management.

Many different agencies are part of the federal government, and each has its own HR functions and management systems, although all are loosely related under the OPM umbrella. That separateness leads to one key problem: achieving unity of effort. In particular, a SSTR operation will require a unified staff working to achieve the goals of the U.S. government, but it will almost certainly be populated by individuals from several departments and agencies, as well as by contractor personnel. The personnel system supporting each SSTR operation must work with the same unity of effort as the country team deployed on the mission.

In view of the issues that surfaced during our interviews, as well as our direct experience with CPA, we chose three basic criteria for evaluating options on how to achieve a unity of effort:

1. **Responsiveness to the Ambassador:** The SSTR operation is likely to have small staffs that provide assistance to deployed personnel. The entire HR effort—in Washington, D.C., and deployed on a SSTR operation—must support the Ambassador. The distinguishing characteristic of this criterion is an operational focus.

2. **Capacity and capability:** No single agency will have the breadth of contacts and expertise to recruit the best personnel in every required field. The goal of this criterion is to maximize the use of recruiting capabilities and capacity across the U.S. government.

3. **Accountability:** Having the responsibility for personnel functions spread across all involved departments and agencies with no formal mechanism that assures accountability will lead to shortcomings in finding and fielding high-quality personnel and to accounting for those personnel in theater. Accountability differs from responsiveness, in that *responsiveness* has to do with the ease of coordination between the Ambassador's staff and the

HR organization supporting that staff's needs, whereas *account-ability* has to do with the ability of the HR organization to document and manage the HR functions needed to support the fielded staff, as well as to measure the results of the HR process. To further describe the difference between responsiveness and accountability, an HR organization incapable of recruiting and keeping track of personnel, but that could easily coordinate with the Ambassador's deployed staff, would be viewed as responsive (i.e., without regard to the acceptability of the response) but not accountable. Conversely, an organization capable of managing the HR functions that required more coordination than the small, deployed staff could handle could be accountable but not responsive.

To achieve unity of effort, we consider three models that plausibly could provide a solution. In the first model, one agency is responsible for the personnel-management effort for the entire operation. In the second, one agency is the lead, supported by the other agencies supplying personnel to the SSTR effort. In the third, recruiting is decentralized, with the agencies responsible for specific billets validating and filling them as needed, but without central HR direction or control.

Before discussing each model, we want to draw attention to the importance of a few factors, alluded to in earlier discussions, which concern primarily permanent federal civil service personnel.

Who pays for personnel salaries is important. For example, if employees are provided to a SSTR operation on a *reimbursable basis* (meaning that personnel costs are borne by the operation's budget) rather than on a *nonreimbursable basis* (meaning that the agency to which the personnel belong is responsible for personnel costs), agencies may be more willing to provide personnel and to have their personnel managed by another agency. A second issue is equitable and consistent personnel policies, such as those for overtime, bonuses, other compensation, promotion, and the like. As mentioned earlier in this chapter, ideally the U.S. government should try to minimize disparities in these policies (e.g, have universal rules) to encourage U.S. government personnel to participate and to protect those who do. A third issue is personnel accountability—in particular, the databases and procedures used to account for personnel from recruitment though redeployment. Centralized systems were absent in the CPA case, and personnel accountability was not done well.[8]

The first model, in which one agency's personnel system is responsible for the entire effort, aligns most closely with the effort in the field (responsiveness). Just as success in a SSTR operation is linked to the responsiveness of all deployed personnel and programs to the designated official leading the effort (hereafter, the Ambassador), so too should the support systems in the United States be responsible to him or her. In particular, this model would permit the Ambassador's deployed-personnel section to reach back to one agency's personnel system, which would manage the processes that ensure documentation, validation, and recruiting for needed personnel. Similarly, it would simplify accountability, because all responsibility would reside with one agency. However, it would not be as strong in recruiting personnel for all required specialties as the other two options.

The second model, in which a lead agency is supported by the personnel systems of all involved agencies, aligns more closely with the requirements to find and retain people with specific expertise while retaining responsibility in one organization for responsiveness and accountability. For example, the Department of Health and Human Services' personnel system in all likelihood would have more success at identifying and recruiting personnel to help rebuild another country's public health system than would the Department of State. This observation generalizes to all specific technical skills. However, while retaining responsibility for all functions in one agency, the work would be done by many. To achieve unity of effort and be responsive to the Ambassador, a lead agency would need to be the central point for documenting, validating, and filling positions. In particular, a SSTR operation's personnel section, to have any control at all of the system, would need

---

[8] Special Inspector General for Iraq Reconstruction, *Audit Report: Management of Personnel Assigned to the Coalition Provisional Authority, Baghdad, Iraq,* Arlington, Va.: Office of the Inspector General, Coalition Provisional Authority, Report Number 04-002, June 25, 2004.

to be able to reach back to a single agency that would manage the tasks required for documenting, validating, and recruiting personnel.

The options above suffer from the drawback that many personnel filling billets in a SSTR operation will be seconded from federal departments and agencies, and these departments and agencies may be reluctant to give up control of their personnel to a single, or lead, agency. Further, the parent agencies would still be responsible for some aspects of deployed personnel's human-resources functions (e.g., retirement, family health benefits). Specifically, the challenges of managing personnel from several parent agencies could be compounded significantly if a single department or agency were to have control of personnel from across the government for significant periods (for a single long, or several shorter, periods)—especially if well-crafted policies are not in place before the operation begins. Accountability would likely remain dispersed across parent agencies, in part because those agencies would have long-term commitments to their personnel.

Finally, we consider the status quo, or third, model, in which billets are assigned to departments and agencies, which individually manage their personnel to fill these billets without central direction from the Ambassador or the lead agency for the operation. This model would require the SSTR organization to coordinate with many departments and agencies across government, and it would therefore pose significant problems in responsiveness and accountability.

Our team assessment of each option based on the three criteria (responsiveness, capacity and capability, and accountability) casts doubt on the effectiveness of the third model (see Figure 4.1). The figure illustrates that the decentralized model, which is effectively the status quo, is not viable. In particular, without a single or lead agency, the U.S. government response is likely to be *ad hoc* and lead to significant problems. If the United States ever again undertakes a SSTR operation requiring a large civilian staff and finds itself inventing, on the fly, the systems by which such a staff will be created and populated, the likely result will be significant waste of resources and, potentially, of lives.

Further, the requirement to be able to recruit for a complete spectrum of skills makes a single-agency model problematic. The Defense Department would be able to do a reasonable job of recruiting across all needed skill sets—DoD runs a large school system, health systems, commercial transportation systems, city-sized military bases with a full spectrum of services, and so forth. However, it would not be as capable in other areas, such as recruiting diplomats. Other departments or agencies might not be as capable. The second model comes out best according to our criteria, although the model has some shortcomings in the realm of accountability. These assessments are summarized in Figure 4.1.

A key component of strategic alignment is *workforce planning*, which OPM defines as follows: "The organization identifies the human capital required to meet organizational goals, conducts analyses to identify competency gaps, develops strategies to address human capital needs and close competency gaps and ensures the organizationis appropriately structured." As articulated in Chapter Two, workforce planning in Iraq was neither rigorous nor particularly effective. Personnel requirements articulated by senior advisors were seldom validated or reviewed in an organizational context. Because workforce require

Figure 4.1
Assessment of Personnel-Management Models

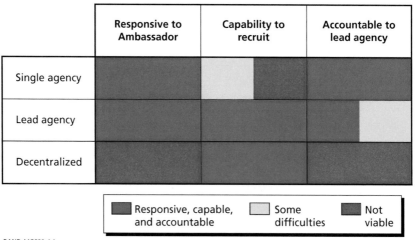

ments and competencies were not identified clearly, the task of recruiting individuals with the technical skills and competencies needed to accomplish organizational goals was more difficult than it should have been. Personnel assessment consisted largely of word-of-mouth referrals and recommendations rather than use of structured assessment tools and conduct of qualifications reviews, which more effectively might have identified true A-Team members.

More importantly, the hard work needed to determine what type of organization would be needed—analogous to what the military calls a *force generation process*, which looks at requirements and determines how the organization that meets the challenge should be structured—was not done. Because it was not done, no demands were placed on the personnel system that would have caused it to fulfill the personnel needed for the CPA.

The failure of the U.S. government policy community to engage government personnel managers in both the planning phase and the execution of the operation in Iraq points to areas in which improvements can be made. Had the CPA structure been created so that it placed well-articulated, strategically aligned demands on the personnel systems of applicable agencies (e.g., security officials on DoD, advisors to the Ministry of Education on the U.S. Department of Education, advisors to the Ministry of Labor and Social Affairs on the U.S. Department of Labor), performance would likely have been much better. The capability to find and field such personnel exists in the personnel systems of the various U.S. government departments and agencies. Accordingly, structure and process matter when establishing civilian staffs, and planning for both standing capabilities and individual operations should involve personnel managers able to advise policymakers.

Likewise, we need to know what type of workforce planning would be needed to place only those demands for maximizing performance on U.S. government personnel systems. One way to envision the problem clearly is to think of a staffing plan, which we will call a *joint manning document*, or JMD (following common DoD usage) based on a well-thought-out workforce plan. Such a pre-prepared JMD should be a product of deliberate planning, which takes place as a normal and formal function carried out by the lead U.S. agency for SSTR operations—S/CRS—and those agencies that support it. It articulates anticipated demand and ought to represent a core set of skills and expandable numbers of billets that are dependent on the situation. In it, there would be two designated types of billets:

- permanent positions authorized to be filled
- permanent positions that are not authorized to be filled unless needed for a specific operation.

An analysis of a proposed JMD, or the collected set of JMDs for all planned operations, should determine which billets fall into which categories. In addition, planners should expect that there will be a third type of position that they will have to deal with—

- unanticipated positions (i.e., those not on the books of any department or agency) created as part of an effort to expand capabilities. These could be either additional positions of known type (i.e., with existing position descriptions) or requirements for people with unanticipated skills that create demand for new kinds of positions. These would most likely be for a looming or existing operation.

These billets are depicted in Figure 4.2, which shows the permanent positions with authority to be filled (Billets 1, 2, and 3) as being filled by civil servants from departments or agencies of the U.S. government. Some of these personnel might be permanently assigned to the designated billets—for example, Department of State personnel assigned to S/CRS. Others could be personnel in agencies designated to fill a particular billet—for example, members of the response or technical corps—who know that they will deploy on an operation, if needed.

Recall that the current S/CRS proposed structure is not sufficient for operational needs beyond small, multinational efforts, and so structures and arrangements may be needed. We will assume that the personnel filling these billets make up the professional cadre of the other

Figure 4.2
Flowchart of Supply of Personnel and Demand for Personnel in the Planning Mechanism Represented by the Joint Manning Document Depiction of Billet Types

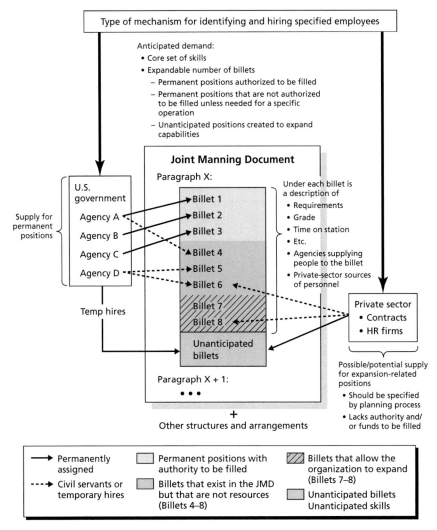

RAND MG580-4.2

U.S. government structure to conduct SSTR operations (e.g., the personnel assigned to S/CRS or offices such as the International Crime Investigative Training Assistance Program [ICITAP] in other U.S. government departments and agencies that play a role in SSTR operations), and, accordingly, these billets are filled by the normal working of the government personnel systems.

Billets 4 through 8 in the figure are those that exist on the JMD but are not resourced, and so are not filled until needed. Although not filled on a day-to-day basis, they are documented and validated, and assigned to a particular agency to fill when the need arises. The dashed arrows from a particular agency to a particular billet indicate that the agency is assigned to fill a particular billet with civil servants or temporary hires should the need arise. Billets 7 and 8 indicate the need to plan for the organization to be expandable. These billets would be described and validated, contingent upon need. They differ from Billets 4 through 6 in that Billets 4 through 6, while also unfunded, would be funded if a deployment occurred, whereas Billets 7 and 8 would not be funded unless additional billets of this type were required.

Finally, the arrows from the private-sector box to Billets 4 through 8 are meant to indicate that not all billets need be filled by civil servants or temporary hires identified by the government, but that some could be contracted for, and others, although temporary hires processed by the appropriate federal government agency, could be identified with the help of outside human-resources firms.[9] These positions are planned for, have the advantage of being on the books of some federal department or agency, and only lack the authority and funds to be filled. Examples might be billets for translators for a particular language who would be required if a SSTR operation took place in a particular area of the world, or specialists in creating banking structures in developing countries. This type of position could be for either a government or contract employee to augment an existing government structure, as is often done in federal government offices, particularly DoD.

In any case, the type of mechanism for identifying and hiring employees (government personnel system or contract) should be speci-

---

[9] For example, this might be necessary if a specialty is needed for which the federal government has no particular expertise or if specific talents are difficult to find.

fied to the degree possible in the planning process and documented in the JMD.

The third type of positions are unanticipated and temporary (i.e., those not on the books of any department or agency). These billets could be of two types. The first type is made up of additional positions of a known kind (e.g., translators), in which case there would be an existing job description (documentation), and the personnel system would only need to validate the requirement before hiring someone to fill it. The second type of position is for an unanticipated skill, in which case there would be no job description at all and the positions would need to be both documented and validated.

If these billets were created as part of an existing organization, then the bureaucratic machinery of that organization would make the task of documenting and validating these positions easier; however, if part of an *ad hoc* structure, documentation and validation would likely be significantly more difficult tasks unless planning had already taken place. Because we are not aware of any plans to create large numbers of deployable billets in S/CRS, we will assume the latter case.

The lessons learned from previous U.S. and UN SSTR efforts should make the task of creating "off-the-shelf" job descriptions reasonable,[10] and, as these lessons learned are translated into concrete planning, the number of unanticipated billets will be reduced.

For temporary positions that were not anticipated, it is likely that no job description would exist until the need was identified—either in the planning for, or actual execution of, a SSTR operation. The demand here would likely be for the rapid identification of someone to fill a billet that could be a government or outsourced position, depicted in Figure 4.2 by the solid "Temp hires" (Temporary Hires) arrow leading from the U.S. government box and the solid arrow from the private-sector box.

It is useful to note that Figure 4.2 is, in many ways, an expansion of Figure 3.2 ("Supply of and Demand for Personnel"). The supply of

---

[10] A great deal of accumulated experience resides with civilians in SSTR operations, including the lessons learned with the Provincial Reconstruction Teams in Iraq and Afghanistan, and experience with similar formations in the Balkans in the 1990s.

personnel, depicted on the left of Figure 3.2, is represented in Figure 4.2 by the "U.S. Government" and "Private Sector" boxes. The demand on the right of Figure 3.2 is captured in the billets on the JMD. Since these billets are fully described and validated, they would capture the functional requirements and characteristics outlined in the earlier figure. Finally, the JMD and our discussion of the mechanics of government personnel systems, as well as the authorities outlined in the first section of this chapter, go far to fill in the question mark in Figure 3.2. We return to this issue in the next chapter, in which we make specific recommendations for standing up this or a similar structure.

The federal government hires personnel through the aforementioned personnel systems of each department or agency, under authorities granted them by law and rules set by regulation. It is worth noting that the federal personnel systems, which exist separately in each department or agency, often with authorities unique to those departments and agencies, are structured to fill requirements in large, mostly permanent organizations and, while they have some capability to respond to quick-turnaround requirements, are not focused on filling large numbers of temporary billets and generally do not have the intrinsic surge capacity that might be needed to staff a quickly evolving SSTR operation.

However, government personnel systems are not the only potential suppliers of personnel. When a private-sector company needs to hire a person with a certain set of skills and qualifications, it often goes to outside personnel firms, such as headhunter firms or Internet sites that keep databases of resumes. One method for recruiting civilian personnel would be to identify a specific organization or organizations within the government or the private sector that could specialize in finding personnel with the unique characteristics (i.e., A-Team characteristics) and functional capabilities needed to run a SSTR operation. The required response times for finding such individuals might vary considerably, from a few weeks for the initial tranche of SSTR operators deploying in the wake of a military intervention to a year or more for the subsequent rotations of personnel in an existing operation.

In the private sector, these firms survive by maintaining databases of personnel who fit the profile of their customers' needs. Such databases enable them to quickly identify and proffer candidates for available positions. This same capability could be hired (thus creating a market for this service if one does not exist) or created within the U.S. government. To some extent, this market already exists, since the UN, International Financial Institutions (IFIs), NGOs, and others rely on those who maintain databases of people willing to deploy as needed, not to mention commercial solutions, such as Monster.com and other Internet-based solutions. Alternately, the U.S. government could outsource some portion of the effort completely to firms that supply qualified people. Many U.S. government departments and agencies hire personnel for routine functions this way, and such firms probably would be able to provide personnel for SSTR operations.

Finally, billets, either identified, authorized, or none of these, could be filled with personnel from allies, coalition partners, or state and local governments. As mentioned previously, there are areas important to SSTR operations in which the federal government does not have particular expertise resident in any of its departments or agencies. For example, the primacy in the United States for such critical skills as police, health, transportation, and education is with state or local authorities, not with the federal government. However, this is not the case in many countries. The billets requiring these functions could be coded so that the preferred approach would be to have an ally or coalition partner that has this expertise in its national government to perform these functions and fill these billets. Billets of these types would be found in such critical areas as education, public health, and transportation.

However, in situations in which no allies or coalition partners were willing or able to fill these billets, the federal government could turn to state and local governments for help. Such reliance would likely require that standing relationships, if not agreements, be established with these governments and the nationwide organizations that represent them (e.g., National Governors Association), in order to make the recruitment and placement of these personnel go smoothly when the need arose. The federal government could even pay for additional billets in some state and local governments, with the understanding (under solution three, contracts with public or private individuals or companies) that those in the federally funded billets would be available for deployment when called.[11]

Leadership and Knowledge Management

For this element, the Framework asks whether agency leaders effectively manage people, ensure continuity of leadership, and sustain a learning environment that drives continuous performance improvement by identifying and addressing gaps in effective leadership and implementing and maintaining programs that capture organizational knowledge and promote learning. The outcome of these efforts is key to providing a constant flow of leaders who can properly direct SSTR operations. However, responsibility for developing a cadre of such leaders appropriately falls to departments and agencies, because a SSTR will often involve temporary organizations that cannot be expected to institutionalize such efforts.

Accordingly, the Departments of State and Defense have each begun to address the types of leadership and continuity gaps that were articulated by many of our interviewees. For example, the State Department's Strategic Plan for 2007 indicates that the Department will increase the percentage of language-designated positions at overseas missions filled by people who fully meet language requirements and will mandate leadership and management training for 100 percent of its targeted population.[12] DoD has announced an initiative to develop 21st-century leaders who will have diverse experiences and competency in "joint matters."[13] The success of these and other related leadership initiatives will increase the capacity of the United States to manage future SSTR operations effectively.

---

[11] See Kelly (2006) for an exposition of how such an approach might work for transitional law-enforcement capabilities.

[12] U.S. Department of State and U.S. Agency for International Development, "Strategic Goal Chapter 12: Management and Organizational Excellence," *FY 2007 Joint Performance Summary*, Washington, D.C., no date.

[13] Marilee Fitzgerald, Office of the Under Secretary of Defense, Civilian Personnel Policy, "The Department of Defense Initiative: Developing 21st Century Senior Executive Service Leaders," Defense Human Resources Board Briefing, August 30, 2006.

Results-Oriented Performance Culture

A *results-oriented performance culture* system "focuses on having a diversity oriented, high-performing workforce, as well as a performance-management system that effectively plans, monitors, develops, rates and rewards employee performance."[14] To be successful, the system must include effective communication, written performance plans that stress measurable results and expectations, documented appraisals, an awards policy, and a pay-for-performance program.

We found little indication of a formal performance management program at the CPA, nor did we find any formal differentiation between high and low performers—not surprising, given the very nature of the CPA, the circumstances and conditions in which it operated, and the relatively brief tenure of most employees.

In thinking about future operations, those involved in the planning process must include a performance-management template that lists performance expectations and includes mandatory performance feedback, as well as incentives for excellent performance (bonuses and awards) and consequences for poor performance. Some of these considerations are discussed in the next section.

Talent Management

OPM defines *talent management* as "a system that addresses competency gaps, particularly in mission-critical occupations, by implementing and maintaining programs to attract, acquire, develop, promote, and retain quality talent."[15] Returning to our initial workforce-planning question, "What capabilities does the United States need?" we can point to two essential elements for creating a functional civilian staff:

---

[14] Consider U.S. Office of Personnel Management, "The Results-Oriented Performance Culture System," *Human Capital Assessment and Accountability Framework (HCAAF) Resource Center*, no date.

[15] U.S. Office of Personnel Management, "The Talent Management System," *Human Capital Assessment and Accountability Framework (HCAAF) Resource Center*, no date.

- the structure and processes required for any staff to function
- qualified personnel to fill the positions on that staff.

Our primary focus in the following discussion falls on the second of these two elements, talent management, with the understanding that the first element will at times place constraints or demands on the personnel-staffing issue.

To shape this discussion, we found it helpful to identify approaches to talent management specifically for fielding civilian staffs. We present and analyze three approaches. These approaches are neither an exhaustive set of options nor mutually exclusive, but they represent the major approaches that surfaced in the course of our interviews. Some of these options may require changes in current laws, regulations, and personnel policies. We also describe the government's accountability system that monitors and analyzes the performance of all aspects of human capital management.

Potential Approaches to Talent Management

The U.S. government could field civilian staffs by

1. requiring U.S. government civilian employees to deploy on SSTR operations as needed
2. providing sufficient incentives to cause civilians in the public and private sectors to volunteer for deployments
3. establishing standing contracts with public- and private-sector civilians or private companies for deployment on SSTR operations.

We describe what each approach involves, in turn.

Requiring U.S. government civilian employees to deploy. This approach, if applied broadly to the U.S. government civilian workforce, would likely have negative effects.[16] Most civilian government workers do not expect to be deployed to austere and dangerous places.

---

[16] Interview with senior U.S. Army civilian personnel manager, July 6, 2005. Interview with senior OPM official November 16, 2005.

Even if laws and regulations permitted this approach, which they do for FSOs and some DoD positions, the decision to assign large numbers of civilian employees involuntarily could have a major negative effect on governmentwide recruiting and retention, and that effect would have to be considered before such actions are taken. In fact, the State Department's consideration of involuntary assignments of FSOs to Iraq has led to speculation that such a move might hurt morale in the Foreign Service, the only civilian institution with the clear authority to make such assignments.[17]

However, this approach could be useful for addressing specific requirements (e.g., key leaders, special skills). If those requirements fit under the criteria for Emergency-Essential personnel of United States Code, Title 10, Section 1580, then a clear and accepted method exists within DoD for making such assignments. Similar legislation could permit personnel managers to make assignments to SSTR staffs of other critical specialties that might exist in DoD as well as in other departments and agencies. Furthermore, in conjunction with the third approach discussed below, domestic staffing could be structured such that those holding certain billets would understand that they were eligible for and required to be assigned to SSTR operations, if the need arose. For example, some billets requiring country and area experts, as well as experts in certain technical skills, could have as one criterion of employment that the person holding that position be subject to involuntary deployment on SSTR operations. Various incentives, discussed below, could be used to attract quality personnel to these positions.

The assignment of large numbers of U.S. government civilian personnel to unusual, atypical overseas missions also has significant implications for the operations of government offices in the United States. Care would be needed to ensure that SSTR deployments caused no U.S. government office to lose too many personnel at once, lest the efficiency of that office, and perhaps of the larger agency to which it belongs, be endangered.

---

[17] Paul Richter, "State Dept. Considers Mandatory Iraq Tours," *Los Angeles Times*, December 18, 2005.

In other words, there would be multiple staffing problems that would need to be managed concurrently: of the SSTR effort and of ensuring that contributing domestic offices were able to function after giving up staff members for the overseas effort. An approach to dealing with these conflicting needs will be addressed under the next option.

Providing sufficient incentives to cause civilians in the public and private sectors to volunteer for deployments. Personnel who worked for private contractors in Iraq earned much more than did government employees with similar jobs, because they were hired and deployed according to market principles, not government pay scales. For example, it was not unusual for the members of a Personal Security Detachment (PSD) for a CPA senior executive to have salaries significantly larger than that of the person they were guarding.[18] This disparity raises the question of what could be done with incentives, although it contradicts the previous discussion about the possibility for disparate benefits causing friction on staffs. The cases for private- and public-sector civilians are sufficiently different to require different approaches, each presented below.

Based on our discussions with executives from the private sector who served on the CPA staff and those charged with recruiting them, incentives could only reasonably be used for junior- and mid-level positions. Executives with private for-profit firms would not be enticed by government salaries or by any benefits that the government would likely be able to offer, especially for temporary positions for which long-term retirement and health insurance coverage is not possible. To paraphrase the words of one such official who served with the CPA as a senior advisor, he was in effect donating his time while in Iraq, even though he was receiving the maximum allowable salary for a government senior executive.[19] This same senior executive thought incentives might work for junior- and mid-level personnel, although doing so could provide them with salaries disproportionately larger than those of their public-sector peers in a SSTR deployment.

---

[18] Based on discussions Kelly had with PSD personnel in Baghdad in 2004.

[19] Interview with former senior CPA official, March 2005.

Incentives for public-sector employees are more likely to provide good results, or at least would not suffer from the same large-scale disparities between market and government salaries that appear at the upper levels of the senior executives. As already discussed, the U.S. government personnel system has the ability to provide several types of incentives to civilians willing to deploy. These include relocation and retention incentives, danger pay, and a foreign-post differential. Furthermore, personnel who deploy should have at least as good a chance of getting an annual performance bonus as they would if they did not deploy, and considerations for promotions should be handled on the same basis. In particular, explicit or implicit penalties for deployment will adversely affect the U.S. ability to staff SSTR operations, and eliminating them is essential.

One overall impression from our interviews of public- and private-sector personnel who deployed with the CPA, as well as the authors' experiences with the CPA, was that most CPA staff members' primary motivation was not monetary. Patriotism and the desire to be part of something important seem to have been the major factors in why many people volunteered to serve in Iraq. Personnel managers need to factor such inclinations into their recruiting and retention plans.

Establishing standing contracts with public- and private-sector civilians or private companies for deployment on SSTR operations. The third approach establishes contractual agreements that collectively fulfill anticipated requirements to provide personnel as needed. For federal employees, this option overlaps with the two previous solutions in that employment contracts can be associated with specific billets, requiring individuals in such billets to deploy as needed in a manner similar to the military National Guard and Reserve concept. Such contracts could include various incentives beyond those discussed above (which addressed incentives that would be forthcoming upon deployment). Examples of monetary incentives might include specialty pay, perhaps modeled after the flight pay given to military pilots and the language pay given to personnel who maintain proficiency in needed languages.

Furthermore, if career tracks were developed in federal departments and agencies for personnel willing to deploy on SSTR operations in any given agency, some of these incentives could be applied on the basis of participating in this career track, because the individual would be doing more than simply filling a particular billet.

Again, flight pay is a good example. Military pilots receive flight pay even when not in a position that requires them to fly, so long as they meet certain qualifying criteria.

Nonmonetary incentives could also be used to recruit and retain personnel in deployable billets or a career track that provided for as-needed deployment. For example, providing regular intelligence briefings and access to information about hot spots in the world could be one element of an incentives package that would appeal to some.

Contracts with individuals and companies in the private sector are other means of securing needed personnel. As mentioned earlier, standing contracts are one method being pursued by S/CRS and the UK PCRU for acquiring needed personnel. The UN and many NGOs, for example, do not maintain large staffs for their operations; rather, they acquire them on an as-needed basis from lists of people with the requisite skills and willingness to deploy that they or other organizations maintain. Standing contracting authority, existing resources, and ready-to-use contract mechanisms would greatly facilitate this approach, as would consideration of a "ready reserve" composed of recently retired federal employees who would agree to being recalled for SSTR operations, again similar to the military National Guard and Reserve concept.

S/CRS has sponsored work, via Joint Forces Command, with the Institute for Defense Analyses, to investigate the viability of creating a civilian response corps for SSTR efforts. This comprehensive study examined several approaches for creating such a corps, organized into a reserve that could deploy given sufficient lead time.[20] These approaches included managed rosters and centralized individual recruiting, pre-arranged contractual agreements, capabilities-based planning systems, and assets on standby. For each of these approaches, IDA reviewed several applicable models and chose as a template or framework for their recommendations the National Wildfire Coordination Group.

---

[20] IDA Briefing given to Terrence Kelly, October 24, 2005.

This group mobilizes large numbers of firefighters every year. Its inter-agency system documents skills and position needs, maintains a data-base of over 70,000 firefighters and support personnel, runs a resource-ordering and -support system, and relies on its national interagency mobilization guide to get firefighters into the system and to the places they are needed.

Realistically, no single solution will fill the needs of the United States in all SSTR operations that can be anticipated, particularly those in which the United States makes substantial personnel contribu-tions. Rather, using the Human Capital Assessment and Accountabil-ity Framework categories of Strategic Alignment and Workforce Plan-ning, planners would be able to determine the talent required, identify recruitment sources, consider the pros and cons and costs of each, and develop an action plan. For example, the costs of maintaining large bodies of people in a deployable status who may not be needed on a reg-ular basis mean that some role will likely be played by nongovernmen-tal civilians, which indicates that a concept of expandability, similar to that that makes necessary the Reserve components of the U.S. military, would be needed. As such, not only are the solution types important to recognize but also are the methods for implementing them. The dis-cussion of potential talent-management solutions for identifying and deploying personnel for SSTR operations should not be understood to apply only to volunteers for *ad hoc* operations and temporary organi-zations, such as those undertaken by the United States recently. These methods are also applicable for identifying personnel to fill identified requirements not needed on a permanent basis.

Accountability

Finally, the HCAAF requires that human capital decisions be guided by a data-driven, results-oriented accountability system that docu-ments the management processes and measures results. Such a system provides a consistent means of monitoring and analyzing the perfor-mance on all aspects of human capital management policies, programs, and activities, which must support mission accomplishment and be effective, efficient, and in compliance with merit-systems principles.

Such a system was largely lacking in Iraq. In fact, the Secretary of Defense deployed multiple assessment teams to ascertain the "ground truth" with regard to numbers of personnel, finances, and other matters. Earlier in this chapter, we discussed the basic criteria for evaluating options for achieving a unity of effort and presented three models for a personnel system—a single agency, a lead agency, and the decentralized approach used in Iraq. Given federal e-gov initiatives, particularly the integration of personnel and payroll systems, and the migration from 26 Executive Branch federal payroll providers to four qualified providers, future SSTR operations might capitalize on integrated, Web-based personnel systems to manage personnel resources regardless of the model selected.

CHAPTER FIVE

Conclusions and Recommendations

How do all of the pieces fit together? Figure 5.1 shows how.[1] In it, we use the OPM Human Capital Assessment and Accountability Framework and the larger SSTR policymaking machinery as guides; building off this model, we make recommendations. These pieces and how they flow into each other or interconnect are illustrated in Figure 5.1.

Policy and Strategic Direction

The policy block in this figure corresponds to national-level policy—specifically, foreign, defense, and SSTR policies, as well as policies on other related topics. Collectively, these policies provide strategic direction to those charged with SSTR planning and operations, for creating the institutional pieces needed to implement these policies.

One key item with regard to the development of policy and strategic direction discussed in the preceding chapters is the need for policymakers to consult with HR and resource managers to ensure that policies are supportable, and to engage HR and resource organizations in support of policy.

---

[1]   In the discussion that follows, we will primarily address the institutional elements of the HCAAF. Those elements that are naturally within the domain of line leadership, such as large portions of the need to create a performance culture, are not discussed explicitly.

Figure 5.1
Fitting the Pieces Together

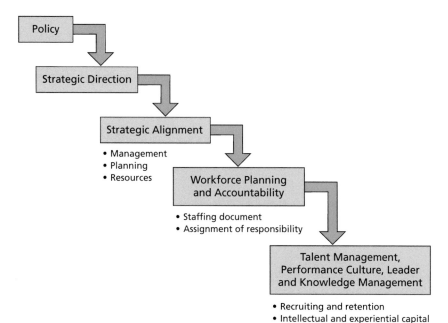

RAND *MG580-5.1*

Recommendation:

- Policymakers should include HR and resource managers during the policymaking phase to ensure that proposed policies are executable and that HR and resource organizations actively support efforts to implement policy.

Strategic Alignment

Our focus begins with the HR Strategic Alignment element from the OPM Human Capital Assessment and Accountability Framework.

Management

Our discussion in Chapter Four of how the effort should be managed falls into the Strategic Alignment category. In that discussion, as illustrated in Figure 4.1, it became clear that orchestrating the HR effort will require a major management effort. The failures of the CPA HR function are replete with lessons to be learned. Among those lessons is the inability of a small, deployed HR staff to coordinate HR functions from the field and the likely consequences of *ad hoc* efforts to field a functional staff. We considered three potential management models:

- Designate one agency to handle all HR functions.
- Designate a lead agency and give it authority to coordinate across the federal government.
- Leave HR functions decentralized.

From our research, we learned that the CPA experience demonstrated that the decentralized methods used for the CPA were not effective. Without significantly reorganizing such a decentralized system, those methods would not be likely to produce good results. However, the principle of unity of effort is as important here as it is in military operations. The difficulties inherent in getting large bureaucracies to work are compounded as accountability is dispersed across agencies. Accordingly, the third model is simply not a viable solution.

Unity of effort is most likely if one agency is given the overall task, but it would place a significant burden on that one agency's HR office, and it is unlikely that any one agency would have the contacts and internal systems in place to recruit all functions needed for a large SSTR operation. Additionally, since many civil servants from across agencies will be taking part in any large-scale operation, routine HR problems will need to be managed by their home agencies while they are deployed. We therefore conclude that the lead-agency option, if properly empowered and resourced, has the greatest likelihood of providing unity of effort and the broad range of skills required in a SSTR operation. That lead agency could be a federal department or agency with an operational mission related to SSTR (e.g., State, DoD) or OPM.

This finding raises the question: Which agency should lead the HR component of SSTR planning and operations? While the State Department has the overall policy lead for SSTR according to

NSPD 44,[2] a definitive answer to that question requires further analysis. Both DoD and the State Department have accumulated many lessons from the recent efforts in Afghanistan and, particularly, in Iraq. Furthermore, since any effort would require the participation of several departments and agencies, OPM should be involved as the principal federal government agency charged with personnel policy across government.

Finally, the HR management structure will need to be able to work across agency boundaries and support U.S. policy, planning, and operations. Therefore, the White House staff—the NSC staff and OMB in particular—should be involved in making decisions about how the effort will be managed and resourced, among other issues. For purposes of implementation of the concept, the formation of specific HR cells dealing with SSTR staff planning at the relevant departments and agencies might be in order. Given the expertise on SSTR operations in DoD, liaisons from DoD at these departments and agencies might be required.

For the lead-agency concept to go forward, legislative action will be needed. If the pace of congressional action in 2005–2006 toward the planning of and funding for SSTR operations is taken as an indication of the contentiousness of the issue, then it is clear that there remain basic differences on how to approach the issue in Congress.[3] It is also our basic observation that the conditions that will necessitate U.S. participation in future SSTR operations remain and that, unless the current *ad hoc* processes for providing civilian staffs for SSTR operations change, there is bound to be much waste in resources and endangering of lives.

---

[2] This conclusion stems from the fact that SSTR operations are civilian-led, and the staffs to which we are referring are civilians with expertise that resides at the State Department and its agencies (USAID).

[3] Nina M. Serafino and Martin A. Weiss, *Peacekeeping and Conflict Transitions: Background and Congressional Action on Civilian Capabilities*, Washington, D.C.: Congressional Research Service, CRS Report for Congress RL32862, June 2, 2006.

Recommendations:

- The President should direct the NSC staff and OPM to cochair a SSTR panel to validate the lead-agency concept, and to determine, among other things, who should lead SSTR HR planning and operations support. At a minimum, the panel should also have senior HR and policy representatives from the Departments of State and Defense, and a representative from S/CRS and from the Office of Management and Budget. This panel should consider planning and operations as two distinct phases of the SSTR effort, and it should explicitly consider the possibility that different management paradigms might be needed for each.
- After considering the recommendations of this panel, and if it validates the lead-agency recommendation, the President should designate one agency as the HR lead for SSTR efforts and give that agency the authority to coordinate across the federal government on all SSTR-related planning and operational HR issues. The President should task the Stability and Reconstruction Operation Policy Coordinating Committee (SRO PCC) with overseeing this process and should be prepared to task departments and agencies in support of this effort. The President may need congressional support in order for this action to receive the proper backing across governmental departments and agencies.

Planning

The planning tasks discussed here are those having to do primarily with structuring the HR effort, not workforce planning. The lead HR office should develop this plan so that, when needed, the SSTR HR function can implement plans smoothly. These plans should include not only the mechanisms by which the lead HR office will coordinate workforce and operational planning with the other applicable agencies of the federal government, but also how the operational HR effort will function. Such considerations as databases to account for deployed personnel, what HR capabilities should be deployed with the operational component of the HR effort (e.g., rear and forward HR staff composition), and use of private-sector HR firms for recruiting might be considered. These are standard issues, many of which will be situation-dependent. We limit ourselves to one recommendation under this topic.

Recommendation:

- The lead HR office, in conjunction with appropriate SSTR policy offices, should conduct formal planning to ensure that it can support SSTR efforts in operational planning and support.

Resources

The U.S. government HR systems did not adequately support the CPA, in large part because they were not engaged in a way that caused them to recruit the right personnel. Part of this failure was slow appropriations of funds for the operations. Additionally, deployed civil servants encountered a myriad of problems with getting permission from their home offices to deploy and with receiving normal benefits such as overtime pay. As well, there were the potential problems that could be caused by disparate benefits packages for personnel from different agencies or even offices within the same department or agency: Individual departments and agencies, and even individual offices, had to absorb the personnel cost of deployed personnel with no offset or reimbursement. For example, a small office that permitted a staff member to deploy for a year might not have the resources to hire a temporary replacement.

These problems, as well as those having to do with hiring and deploying temporary employees, would have been alleviated to a great extent had there been a central authority to hire and pay personnel costs and had the funds to do so been immediately available. The Stafford Act provides a good example of how such arrangements could be made. Under the Stafford Act,[4] specified U.S. government departments

---

[4] *Wikipedia* describes the Robert T. Stafford Disaster Relief and Emergency Assistance Act, Public Law 100-707, as "a United States federal law to bring an orderly and systematic means of federal natural disaster assistance to state and local governments in carrying out their responsibilities to aid citizens."

and agencies have the authority to take personnel actions and spend from a standing fund upon a declaration of need by the President.

Recommendations:

- The President should request, and Congress should authorize, standing authority to recruit SSTR personnel and pay related personnel costs, subject only to an appropriate declaration of need by the President.
- The President should request, and Congress appropriate, funds for the lead agency to handle all personnel costs of SSTR efforts, thus eliminating additional financial burdens on departments and agencies seconding personnel to a SSTR effort.
- The Stafford Act could serve as a model for these authorities and the funding mechanism.

Workforce Planning and Accountability

Workforce planning is part of the larger SSTR planning effort. One could think of the workforce plan as an annex to a larger SSTR plan. Two types of planning are to be considered here: planning the workforce for generic SSTR efforts (discussed in the preceding chapters) and operational planning (not discussed in detail in the preceding chapters). In many regards, the considerations will be the same for each, and we will differentiate between them only as needed.

Workforce planning is the element that would replace the large question mark in the center of Figure 3.2, and result in the production of a JMD (the central component of Figure 4.2). In our JMD discussion, we did not specify who should create the JMD but, rather, used the JMD to motivate the discussion of the types of billets that would naturally be present and their relationship to existing government HR systems. We also argued in two of the preceding chapters that government HR systems have special authorities that permit them to offer significant incentives and to hire people rapidly, that the number of people needed is small relative to the capacity of government HR systems, and that for the government personnel systems to recruit they need fully described positions that have been validated. We also pointed out that, in addition to using existing HR systems, the government could contract with private-sector HR firms to identify people to recruit and could also contract for personnel outside of HR channels. All of these possibilities are dependent on knowing what personnel are needed.

The JMD would capture the results of the workforce-planning effort, combining input from operational and HR experts to provide fully described and validated billets. It should also be flexible enough to accommodate additional billets of known type (Billets 4 through 8 in Figure 4.2) and new types of billets (the "Unanticipated Billets" portion of Figure 4.2). Chapter Four discussed the organizations best suited for recruiting personnel for each billet type.

The preparation for SSTR efforts should include a generic JMD that could be modified for specific operations by adding and subtracting billets as needed—in essence, an off-the-shelf tool that would streamline planning in an emergency. Since a given SSTR effort might not be in an area in which a robust U.S. diplomatic mission exists, the generic JMD should provide for an organization with the capability to stand alone. If planning is thorough and uses a wide range of lessons learned and expert input, most billet types would be identified and included. As lessons learned accumulate, the number of unanticipated billets should decrease.

Recommendations:

- As part of its planning efforts, the S/CRS and the lead HR office should create a generic JMD for a temporary SSTR organization that could operate independent of a U.S. Mission. This JMD should list positions for the operation, using the three types articulated in Chapter Four (validated and resourced; validated but not resourced; and known but not validated). Unanticipated billets would, by definition, not be accounted for in the JMD.
- Planning should include the ability to expand for larger operations and the flexibility to document and quickly validate those positions that are not anticipated.

- Each billet in this JMD should be assigned to a specific agency with a time frame for filling it, or should be designated as a position to be contracted for with an agency responsible for the contracting process.
- The workforce plan should be reviewed by the SRO PCC, which should ensure that HR and resource leaders are part of the process for developing, resourcing, and reviewing the plan. HR and resource managers should also be involved in preparing and executing operations.

Talent Management, Performance Culture, Leader and Knowledge Management

These last three elements of the OPM HCAAF deal with who actually fills what billets, as well as HR and SSTR operational issues. Clear lines of responsibility for filling billets will be critical to the success of the SSTR HR effort. In particular, the planning effort must include an analysis of each billet in the JMD to ensure that the appropriate agency is charged with filling it, and that each agency identifies the type of recruiting needed (e.g., for existing civil servants, temporary hires, contracting).

Moving from the JMD at the center of Figure 4.2 outward, we see that the arrows connect billets, each of which includes a complete description of requirements, grade, time on station, and other aspects of the position, along with agencies charged with supplying the people to fill these billets and private-sector sources of personnel. Table 4.1, which summarizes federal government HR authorities needed for this task, and the discussion that precedes it, describes the tools that managers have to recruit and direct qualified individuals to fill JMD billets. This figure and the discussions in Chapter Four on mechanisms for connecting supply and demand and implementation methods make clear that the U.S. government needs a collection of HR tools that is organized into effective programs under a strong HR management framework.

HR system managers should consider personnel from various sources, such as civil servants, members of state and local governments, and private-sector personnel, as appropriate, for a given billet. A detailed analysis of JMD billets would provide significant amounts of information about which personnel sources are most appropriate for which billets. To do this, consideration should be given to the functional requirements of each position and to where the expertise for identifying those requirements can be found. Second, consideration should be given to which systems have the best chance of recruiting the best personnel. Options include using U.S. government HR systems and contracting with private-sector firms to identify personnel that the U.S. government would hire either as government employees or as contract personnel. These decisions should also be based on an analysis of the JMD billets and the strengths and weaknesses of U.S. government HR systems. Within the U.S. government, consideration should be given to which agency HR systems could find the best people for each billet.

To attract the right people and keep them available for deployment, attention must be paid to inducements and impediments to recruiting and retention. As discussed in Chapter Four, personnel managers have many tools for creating incentives for interested personnel. Furthermore, innovative as well as standard management tools should be considered for this function. For example, the State Department currently keeps a database of retired FSOs who are willing to consider deploying on such operations, and several other databases list private individuals with specific skills who are willing to help with general or specific causes. All such approaches should be considered.

Once people are designated against specific billets on the JMD, care must be given to retaining them, which involves providing training as well as incentives. Training for SSTR operations will be relatively expensive. As well, the ability to operate as an organization will require some continuity on the part of the staff,[5] which means that attention must be paid to identifying and offering inducements for retaining as well as recruiting qualified personnel. The U.S. government has much experience in this field. Military personnel managers routinely offer inducements for dangerous billets, and civilian HR leaders manage workforce composition and strength every day. It is possible that the current authorities, outlined in Chapter Four, would prove insufficient to recruit and retain qualified personnel. To determine whether this is so, a gap analysis should be conducted to identify additional needed authorities, such as the authority to exceed current pay levels or to direct the deployment of the holders of certain government billets. This analysis should take into consideration uncertainty in personnel availability, which would depend on the mission to which they would be deployed and the labor markets from which personnel would be drawn.

Finally, to help ensure that the system works, periodic exercises should be held. The Continuity of Government (COG) and Continuity of Operations (COOP) programs run by the federal government are one set of programs that provides a model of such exercises. Some of the COG and COOP team members work COOP and/or COG full-time; however, most are in billets in which they perform normal department or agency business until called upon in an emergency. In these departments/agencies, staffs designated as part of a COOP or COG team typically walk through the performance of their duties in response to a given scenario. The senior person on each team who would perform a task in a real emergency—usually a very senior person at the SES or Executive Service level—is expected to participate.

Recommendations:

- Responsible agencies should analyze their billets in the JMD to determine what part of society (e.g., federal government, state or

---

[5] Since the civilian staff will need to work closely with military personnel, using some of the military facilities (Fort Polk, Fort Irwin, the National Defense University [NDU], and the Army War College [AWC]) and emphasizing civil-military training might be a cost-effective option.

local government, private sector) would most likely be able to provide people to fill each billet. This analysis should be based primarily on the functional requirements for that billet.

- The lead HR office should render periodic reports to the NSC SRO PCC and OPM on the status of recruiting and retention efforts, providing specific data on the performance of each federal agency charged with filling JMD billets.
- The NSC SRO PCC should designate an agency or office (e.g., OPM, S/CRS) to be responsible for conducting periodic audits of the personnel designated for specific JMD billets, to ensure that they are qualified and remain available
- The lead HR office should analyze JMD billets to identify those in which there is little or no federal expertise, and should plan and, if possible, arrange for other personnel sources (e.g., allied, state, or local governments, or the private sector) to fill them.
- OPM and department/agency regulations should stipulate when a U.S. government office supervisor may and may not hinder the participation of one of his or her employees in SSTR operations.
- From the requirements stipulated in the JMD, the lead HR office should determine what, if any, inducements are required to attract and retain the personnel needed for a strong civilian staff:
  – Standard options, such as signing bonuses, specialty pay, and retirement and promotion benefits, should be considered explicitly.
  – Nonstandard benefits, such as specialty training and access to intelligence on world hot spots (subject to adequate security clearance and a need to know), should also be considered explicitly.
- In light of the above analyses, OPM should compare existing authorities to staffing requirements to determine what, if any, additional authorities or legislation is needed to ensure that recruiting efforts will result in a full, competent staff.
- As part of the task to ensure a performance culture, the NSC SRO PCC and the lead HR office should hold periodic exercises in which SSTR HR personnel simulate the implementation of the workforce plan. These exercises should be attended by those actu-

ally charged with given tasks under the plan, should be observed by OPM, and the results should be presented to the NSC Deputies and Principals Committees. COOP and COG programs provide models after which these exercises could be modeled.

Final Words

One way to describe these recommendations is to revisit Figure 3.2 and incorporate into it the above discussion and recommendations. These recommendations can be summed up by stating that the mechanism that links supply to demand is a well-planned process, at the center of which lies the HCAAF process laid out in Figure 5.1. This layout is depicted simply in Figure 5.2.

Figure 5.2
The Missing Link: HCAAF

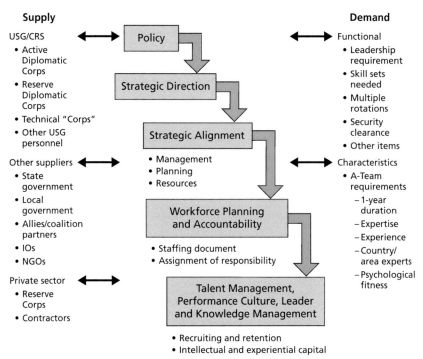

Creating a Civilian Staff in Iraq, 2003–2004

The experience of the Coalition Provisional Authority provides the defining terms of reference for the issues and problems dealt with in this monograph. Therefore, in this Appendix we present a brief overview of U.S.-led efforts to field a civilian staff in Iraq, highlighting the numbers and types of personnel fielded for various operations.

Iraq: Office of Reconstruction and Humanitarian Assistance

On January 20, 2003, President George W. Bush signed National Security Presidential Directive 24 (NSPD-24). It created the Office of Reconstruction and Humanitarian Assistance (ORHA) to rebuild Iraq in the wake of the U.S.-led invasion.

ORHA was charged with ensuring security, stability, and public order for up to two years after U.S. tanks stormed Baghdad; providing transition authority to Iraqi institutions; and transforming the former Ba'athist dictatorship into a democratically elected body that governed under a constitution drafted by representatives of the Iraqi people.[1]

In the early stages of the rebuilding effort, ORHA was composed of about 350 direct- and indirect-support personnel. This crew grew to about 600 staffers while deployed to Kuwait, and it had risen to 1,100 personnel in Baghdad by spring 2004. With the establishment of the

---

[1] Robert M. Perito, *Where Is the Lone Ranger When We Need Him?* Washington, D.C.: United States Institute of Peace Press, 2004, p. 303.

Coalition Provisional Authority (CPA) in May 2003, these numbers increased to more than 6,000 direct and indirect positions—1,200 directly supporting the CPA mission.[2]

ORHA replaced a highly centralized Iraqi bureaucracy that provided all services to the Iraqi people (e.g., education, health care, and transportation services) and that managed the oil and agriculture sectors. The Ba'athist regime discouraged initiative among civil servants. Many of the better administrators had emigrated in the 1980s and 1990s because of repressive state policies and a sharp decline in incomes that accompanied government mismanagement and UN economic sanctions.[3]

The White House first envisioned ORHA as an "expeditionary" unit of civilians that would deploy to Iraq and bring U.S.-style efficiency to a state long plagued by poor bureaucratic management and brutality. Headed by Lieutenant General Jay Garner (U.S. Army, Ret.), ORHA was staffed by personnel on detail from State, Treasury, Energy, Agriculture, Justice, and the U.S. Agency for International Development (USAID). Their overarching job was to coordinate humanitarian assistance and relief, reconstruction, communications, logistics, and budget, often orchestrating work completed by coalition partners, the UN, Nongovernmental Organizations (NGOs), and other institutions.[4]

A mock two-day "rock drill" nearly a month before the invasion of Iraq revealed to LTG Garner that little post-conflict planning had been completed. Garner's expeditionary headquarters nevertheless arrived in Baghdad on April 21, 2003, 12 days after U.S. forces took the city. Most of his 300-member staff, however, arrived "some days later."[5]

ORHA had concentrated its planning on extinguishing oil fires, feeding and housing refugees, stemming mass starvation, and mitigating the devastation of chemical and biological weapons. None of

---

[2] U.S. Government Accountability Office (2004), p. 37.

[3] Dobbins et al. (2005), p. 186.

[4] Perito (2004), p. 304.

[5] Perito (2004), pp. 314–315.

these situations occurred in the large numbers that had been expected. Instead, the 300 ORHA staffers had to contend with a complete collapse of public order and services, crises, as it readily became apparent, that ORHA could not handle.[6]

Few ORHA staffers had ever participated in peace operations, visited Iraq, or spoke Arabic. They had little office equipment and could not receive email or make phone calls indoors. Few staffers realized how hot Iraq would be in the spring and found themselves toiling in Spartan, broiling conditions.

Iraq: Coalition Provisional Authority

The Coalition Provisional Authority replaced ORHA on May 7, 2003. Composed of U.S. and UK citizens, it was given a UN mandate to govern until Iraqi institutions were capable of overseeing daily operations.

President Bush replaced LTG Garner with former Ambassador L. Paul Bremer III, a counterterrorism expert whom the White House hoped would prove a more dynamic and resourceful leader.[7] Three months into the U.S. occupation of Iraq, Bremer's staff had reportedly risen to more than 600 civilians.[8]

As with Garner's ORHA, poor staffing conditions also plagued Bremer's CPA. Former New York City Police Commissioner Bernard Kerik, for example, had to address the Iraqi lawlessness with teams that consisted of only 26 U.S. police advisors from the Department of Justice's International Criminal Investigative Training Program. Kerik's tiny team had to conduct a nationwide needs assessment and develop a plan of action while immediately reconstituting a brutal, corrupt, and poorly educated Iraqi constabulary, plus all the customs, immigration, border patrol, fire, and emergency medical services.[9]

---

[6] Perito (2004), p. 315.

[7] Perito (2004), pp. 315–316.

[8] Romesh Ratnesar, "Life Under Fire," *Time*, Vol. 162, No. 2, July 14, 2003, p. 22.

[9] Perito (2004), pp. 316–319.

Kerik's crew determined that it needed more than 6,600 international police advisors, including 360 professional police trainers destined for Iraqi police colleges and other training facilities—plus another 170 border-control experts—simply to teach a new crop of Iraqi police basic policing and administrative skills. Contracted by the State Department, DynCorp was prepared to take on this task. The CPA waffled on accepting Kerik's recommendations, however, and the project stalled.[10]

The then–General Accounting Office (now known as the Government Accountability Office) summarized the CPA's human-resources challenges in a 2004 report:

- The CPA faced a number of challenges in identifying, obtaining, and organizing the human resources required to help stabilize and reconstruct Iraq.
- The CPA's staffing requirements also changed over time as the mission evolved from a reconstruction and humanitarian effort to the temporary administration of the Iraq government.
- The CPA was dependent on personnel from multiple sources and generally operated with about one-third fewer staff than it required.[11]

The civilian personnel supporting the CPA came from a number of sources: U.S. and coalition employees, contractors, civilians hired under special authorities, and Iraqi expatriates from the Iraq Reconstruction and Development Council (IRDC). The United Kingdom, the Combined Joint Task Force–Seven (CJTF-7), the U.S. Army Corps of Engineers, interpreters, and the American company Kellogg, Brown and Root (KBR) provided indirect support in the form of security, transportation, logistics, maintenance, and translation services.[12]

---

[10] Perito (2004), p. 319; and Seth G. Jones, Jeremy M. Wilson, Andrew Rathmell, and Kevin Jack Riley, *Establishing Law and Order After Conflict*, Santa Monica, Calif.: RAND Corporation, MG-374-RC, 2005, p. 132.

[11] GAO (2004), p. 2.

[12] GAO (2004), p. 37.

Although the total number of CPA personnel fluctuated, the composition of personnel remained consistent:

- The military services provided an average of about 28 percent.
- Approximately 26 percent was civilian detailees from numerous U.S. federal agencies, including the Defense Department (DoD).
- Approximately 13 percent was detailees from other coalition countries.[13]
- About 25 percent was contractors and temporary U.S. government employees hired under a special authority.[14]

The GAO reported that agency officials from the Department of State, USAID, and the Army Corps of Engineers "had relied on volunteers—exclusive of U.S. military personnel—to meet the demand for CPA staff and had not resorted to forced placement (the Secretary of State solicited staff outside of the standard placement process through cables requesting civil and foreign service volunteers for 3-month and, later, 6-month tours)."[15] Table A.1 shows the composition of CPA direct-support personnel from March until June 2004.

The CPA began to reduce personnel in anticipation of the transition of authority to the Iraqis in May 2004. It had a total of 1,050 personnel in Iraq as of June 2004 who directly supported the mission:

> Several elements of the CPA were identified to continue the U.S. effort in Iraq after the transition. According to CPA officials, preliminary plans called for a continued ministry advisory team, a headquarters support group, military and police training teams, and governance teams. An 11 May 2004, National Security Presi-

---

[13] U.S. civilian personnel were detailed to the CPA from various U.S. agencies, including the Departments of Agriculture, Commerce, Energy, Defense, Homeland Security, the Interior, Labor, State, Transportation, the Treasury, Veterans Affairs, the Office of Management and Budget, the National Aeronautics and Space Administration, the U.S. Agency for International Development, the U.S. Postal Service, the U.S. Public Health Service, and the Federal Aviation Administration.

[14] GAO (2004), p. 37.

[15] GAO (2004), pp. 37–38.

dential Directive stated that the U.S. Mission in Baghdad and its temporarily established Iraq Reconstruction Management Office [would] assume those authorities and responsibilities that will continue after the termination of the CPA. The directive also states that the United States Central Command shall continue to be responsible for U.S. security and military operation efforts.[16]

By spring 2004, the security situation in Iraq had deteriorated to the point that the State Department had to revise downward the number of international police experts willing to travel to Iraq. The revised targets were 500 U.S. and 500 non-U.S. professional advisors, plus another 200 international police trainers. In August 2004, however, only 376 U.S. advisors and 57 U.S. trainers were in Iraq, along with about 50 non-U.S. advisors and trainers.[17]

Table A.1
Personnel Composition of Direct CPA Support in Baghdad, March–June 2004

Type of Personnel	03/08/04	04/06/04	05/04/04	06/02/04
Special Hiring Authority 3161	226	237	240	203
Coalition detailees	172	160	141	120
U.S. detailees (not including DoD)	149	208	207	209
DoD military	293	377	326	292
DoD civilian	168	81	88	92
Contractor	62	73	72	66
IRDC	29	27	30	27
Personnel in process	98	76	57	41
Total	1,196	1,239	1,161	1,050

SOURCE: Coalition Provisional Authority, as cited in GAO, *Rebuilding Iraq: Resource, Security, Governance, Essential Services, and Oversight Issues*, Report to Congressional Committees, Washington, D.C.: GAO-04-902-R, June 2004, p. 39.

NOTE: According to CPA officials, the data presented above are about 90 percent accurate, owing to the difficulties of tracking personnel entering and exiting Iraq.

---

[16] GAO (2004), p. 39.

[17] Jones et al. (2005), p. 132.

Also in spring 2004, DoD had decided to take over the CPA's police-training efforts. With a uniformed director and a civilian deputy, members of CJTF-7 came from both the civilian and military ranks. Combined with the Office of Security Cooperation, which was responsible for training the Iraqi Army and later renamed the Multi-National Security Transition Command–Iraq (MNSTC-I), it selects, trains, retains, and equips all Iraqi security forces.[18]

MNSTC-I handed off a number of duties to civilian contractors. To purge and revamp the ranks of the Iraqi Correctional Service (ICS), MNSTC-I transferred operations from military authorities to 107 civilian prison experts, most of whom were retired corrections personnel.[19]

The CPA officially dissolved on June 28, 2004, when it transferred power to a sovereign Iraqi interim government. Since the transition to partial Iraqi government control, U.S. staffing in many departments has shrunk. The CPA, for example, once employed up to 35 expatriate advisors to oversee reformation of the Iraqi Ministry of Justice, including the implementation of a Central Criminal Court and the Iraqi Commission on Public Integrity. After Iraqis assumed control of the Ministry, however, U.S. advisory posts dwindled to 13.[20]

---

[18] Jones et al. (2005), pp. 124–125.

[19] Jones et al. (2005), p. 142.

[20] Jones et al. (2005), p. 141.

Select Bibliography

Binnendijk, Hans, and Stuart Johnson, eds., *Transforming for Stabilization and Reconstruction Operations*, Fort McNair, Washington, D.C.: National Defense University, Center for Technology and National Security Policy, April 2004.

The Clinton Administrations' Policy on Managing Complex Contingency Operations: Presidential Decision Directive, May 1997. As of July 10, 2007:
http://www.fas.org/irp/offdocs/pdd56.htm

Cole, Ronald H., Joint History Office, Office of the Chairman of the Joint Chiefs of Staff, *Operation Just Cause: The Planning and Execution of Joint Operations in Panama, February 1988–January 1990*, Washington, D.C., 1995.

———, *Operation Urgent Fury: The Planning and Execution of Joint Operations in Grenada, 12 October–2 November 1983*, Washington, D.C., 1997.

Crane, Conrad C., and W. Andrew Terrill, *Reconstructing Iraq: Insights, Challenges, and Missions for Military Forces in a Post-Conflict Scenario*, Carlisle Barracks, Pa.: U.S. Army War College, Strategic Studies Institute, 2003.

Dobbins, James, Seth G. Jones, Keith Crane, Andrew Rathmell, Brett Steele, Richard Teltschik, and Anga Timilsina, *The UN's Role in Nation-Building: From the Congo to Iraq*, Santa Monica, Calif.: RAND Corporation, MG-304-RC, 2005. As of January 22, 2007:
http://www.rand.org/pubs/monographs/MG304/

Dobbins, James, John G. McGinn, Keith Crane, Seth G. Jones, Rollie Lal, Andrew Rathmell, Rachel Swanger, and Anga Timilsina, *America's Role in Nation-Building*, Santa Monica, Calif.: RAND Corporation, MR-1753-RC, 2003. As of January 22, 2007:
http://www.rand.org/pubs/monograph_reports/MR1753/

Executive Office of the President, Office of Management and Budget, *The President's Management Agenda, Fiscal Year 2002*, Washington, D.C., no date. As of July 19, 2007:
http://www.whitehouse.gov/omb/budget/fy2002/mgmt.pdf

Fitzgerald, Marilee, Office of the Under Secretary of Defense, Civilian Personnel Policy, "The Department of Defense Initiative: Developing 21st Century Senior Executive Service Leaders," Defense Human Resources Board Briefing, August 30, 2006. As of January 19, 2007:
http://www.cpms.osd.mil/sespm/docs/DHRBAugustBrief-AugustFinal.pdf

GAO—See U.S. Government Accountability Office.

Green, Eric, *New U.N. Mission Assumes Command of Peacekeeping Activities in Haiti*, June 28, 2004. As of October 12, 2005:
http://globalsecurity.org/military/library/news/2004/06/mil-040628-usia02.htm

Jennings, Ray Salvatore, *The Road Ahead: Lessons in Nation Building from Japan, Germany, and Afghanistan for Postwar Iraq*, Washington, D.C.: United States Institute of Peace, April 2003.

Johnson, David E., Karl P. Mueller, and William H. Taft, V, *Conventional Coercion Across the Spectrum of Operations: The Utility of U.S. Military Forces in the Emerging Security Environment*, Santa Monica, Calif.: RAND Corporation, MR-1494-A, 2002. As of January 22, 2007:
http://www.rand.org/pubs/monograph_reports/MR1494/

Jones, Seth G., Jeremy M. Wilson, Andrew Rathmell, and Kevin Jack Riley, *Establishing Law and Order After Conflict*, Santa Monica, Calif.: RAND Corporation, MG-374-RC, 2005. As of January 22, 2007:
http://www.rand.org/pubs/monographs/MG374/

Kelly, Terrence K., *Options for Transitional Security Capabilities for America*, Santa Monica, Calif.: RAND Corporation, TR-353-A, 2006. As of January 22, 2007:
http://www.rand.org/pubs/technical_reports/TR353/

Niblack, Preston, Thomas S. Szayna, and John Bordeaux, *Increasing the Availability and Effectiveness of Non-U.S. Forces for Peace Operations*, Santa Monica, Calif.: RAND Corporation, MR-701-OSD (limited distribution), 1996.

Oakley, Robert B., Michael J. Dziedzic, and Eliot M. Goldberg, eds., *Policing the New World Disorder: Peace Operations and Public Security*, Honolulu, Hawaii: University Press of the Pacific, 2002.

Office of Personnel Management Web site. As of July 12, 2007:
http://apps.opm.gov/HumanCapital/index.cfm

Office of the Under Secretary of Defense for Acquisition, Technology, and Logistics, *Defense Science Board 2004 Summer Study on Transition to and from Hostilities*, Washington, D.C.: U.S. Department of Defense, December 2004.

Oliker, Olga, Richard Kauzlarich, James Dobbins, Kurt W. Basseuner, Donald L. Sampler, John G. McGinn, Michael J. Dziedzic, Adam Grissom, Bruce Pirnie, Nora Bensahel, and A. Istar Guven, *Aid During Conflict: Interaction Between Military and Civilian Assistance Providers in Afghanistan*, September 2001–June 2002, Santa Monica, Calif.: RAND Corporation, MG-212-OSD, 2004. As of January 22, 2007:
http://www.rand.org/pubs/monographs/MG212/

Orr, Robert C., ed., *Winning the Peace: An American Strategy for Post-Conflict Reconstruction*, Carlisle Barracks, Pa.: U.S. Army War College, Center for Strategic and International Studies, July 2004.

Pei, Minxin, and Sara Kasper, *Lessons from the Past: The American Record on Nation Building*, Washington, D.C.: Carnegie Endowment for International Peace, May 2003.

Perito, Robert M., *Where Is the Lone Ranger When We Need Him?* Washington, D.C.: United States Institute of Peace Press, 2004.

Perito, Robert M., Michael Dziedzic, and Beth DeGrasse, *Building Civilian Capacity for U.S. Stability Operations: The Rule of Law Component*, Washington, D.C.: United States Institute of Peace, Special Report 118, April 2004.

Ratnesar, Romesh, "Life Under Fire," *Time*, Vol. 162, No. 2, July 14, 2003.

Richter, Paul, "State Dept. Considers Mandatory Iraq Tours," *Los Angeles Times*, December 18, 2005.

"Robert T. Stafford Disaster Relief and Emergency Assistance Act," *Wikipedia*. As of July 16, 2007:
http://en.wikipedia.org/wiki/Stafford_Disaster_Relief_and_Emergency_Assistance_Act

Roosevelt, Theodore, "'The Man in the Arena' Speech at the Sorbonne, Paris, France, April 23, 1910," *Citizenship in a Republic*. As of July 19, 2007:
http://www.theodore-roosevelt.com/trsorbonnespeech.html

Serafino, Nina M., *Peacekeeping and Related Stability Operations: Issues of U.S. Involvement*, Washington, D.C.: Congressional Research Service, S/CRS Issue Brief for Congress IB94040, September 15, 2005.

Serafino, Nina M., and Martin A. Weiss, *Peacekeeping and Conflict Transitions: Background and Congressional Action on Civilian Capabilities*, Washington, D.C.: Congressional Research Service, CRS Report for Congress RL32862, June 2, 2006.

Shafer, D. Michael, *The Legacy: The Vietnam War in the American Imagination*, Boston, Mass.: Beacon Press, 1990.

Special Inspector General for Iraq Reconstruction, *Audit Report: Management of Personnel Assigned to the Coalition Provisional Authority, Baghdad, Iraq,* Arlington, Va.: Office of the Inspector General, Coalition Provisional Authority, Report Number 04-002, June 25, 2004. As of November 1, 2006: http://www.sigir.mil/reports/pdf/audits/personnel_mgmt.pdf

United Nations, "Eastern Slavonia, Baranja and Western Sirmium: Facts and Figures," 2005a. As of October 13, 2005: http://www.un.org/Depts/dpko/dpko/co_mission/untaes_p.htm

———, "Haiti: Facts and Figures," 2005b. As of October 13, 2005: http://www.un.org/Depts/dpko/dpko/co_mission/unsmihfacts.html

U.S. Department of Defense, Department of Defense Directive 3000.05, Washington, D.C., November 2005.

———, *Personnel Assessment Team Report to the Secretary of Defense,* Washington, D.C., February 2004.

———, *Quadrennial Defense Review Report,* Washington, D.C., February 2006. As of July 10, 2007: http://www.defenselink.mil/pubs/pdfs/QDR20060203.pdf

U.S. Department of State, "Office of the Coordinator for Reconstruction and Stabilization (S/CRS)," briefing to RAND project team, no date.

U.S. Department of State and U.S. Agency for International Development, "Strategic Goal Chapter 12: Management and Organizational Excellence," *FY 2007 Joint Performance Summary,* Washington, D.C., no date. As of January 19, 2007: http://www.state.gov/documents/organization/59182.pdf

U.S. Department of State, Office of the Coordinator for Reconstruction and Stabilization, *Post-Conflict Reconstruction Essential Tasks,* Washington, D.C., April 2005. As of July 10, 2007: http://www.state.gov/documents/organization/53464.pdf

U.S. Department of the Treasury, Office of Performance Budgeting and Strategic Planning, "About the President's Management Agenda." As of July 19, 2007: http://www.treas.gov/offices/management/budget/president_management.shtml/

U.S. Government Accountability Office (GAO), *Rebuilding Iraq: Resource, Security, Governance, Essential Services, and Oversight Issues,* Report to Congressional Committees, Washington, D.C.: GAO-04-902-R, June 2004.

U.S. Joint Forces Command (J7), U.S. Department of State, Office of the Coordinator for Reconstruction and Stabilization, *US Government Draft Planning Framework for Reconstruction, Stabilization, and Conflict Transformation*, Version 1.0, Washington, D.C., December 2005. As of July 18, 2007:
http://www.dtic.mil/doctrine/jel/other_pubs/jwfcpam_draft.pdf

U.S. Office of Personnel Management, *Human Capital Assessment and Accountability Framework*. As of January 18, 2007:
http://www.opm.gov/hcaaf_resource_center/

————, "The Results-Oriented Performance Culture System," *Human Capital Assessment and Accountability Framework (HCAAF) Resource Center*, no date. As of January 28, 2008:
http://www.opm.gov/hcaaf_resource_center/5-1.asp

————, "The Talent Management System," *Human Capital Assessment and Accountability Framework (HCAAF) Resource Center*, no date.
As of January 28, 2008:
http://www.opm.gov/hcaaf_resource_center/6-1.asp

U.S. Office of Personnel Management, Web site. As of July 12, 2007:
www.opm.gov